MznLnx

Missing Links Exam Preps

Exam Prep for

College Math for Business, Economics, Life Sciences & Social Sciences

Barnett, Ziegler, & Byleen, 11th Edition

The MznLnx Exam Prep is your link from the texbook and lecture to your exams.
The MznLnx Exam Preps are unauthorized and comprehensive reviews of your textbooks.

All material provided by MznLnx and Rico Publications (c) 2010
Textbook publishers and textbook authors do not particpate in or contribute to these reviews.

MznLnx

Rico Publications

Exam Prep for College Math for Business, Economics, Life Sciences & Social Sciences
11th Edition
Barnett, Ziegler, & Byleen

Publisher: Raymond Houge
Assistant Editor: Michael Rouger
Text and Cover Designer: Lisa Buckner
Marketing Manager: Sara Swagger
Project Manager, Editorial Production: Jerry Emerson
Art Director: Vernon Lowerui

Product Manager: Dave Mason
Editorial Asitant: Rachel Guzmanji
Pedagogy: Debra Long
Cover Image: Jim Reed/Getty Images
Text and Cover Printer: City Printing, Inc.
Compositor: Media Mix, Inc.

(c) 2010 Rico Publications
ALL RIGHTS RESERVED. No part of this work covered by the copyright may be reproduced or used in any form or by an means--graphic, electronic, or mechanical, including photocopying, recording, taping, Web distribution, information storage, and retrieval systems, or in any other manner--without the written permission of the publisher.

Printed in the United States
ISBN:

For more information about our products, contact us at:
Dave.Mason@RicoPublications.com

For permission to use material from this text or product, submit a request online to:
Dave.Mason@RicoPublications.com

Contents

CHAPTER 1
Linear Equations and Graphs — 1
CHAPTER 2
Functions and Graphs — 9
CHAPTER 3
Mathematics of Finance — 20
CHAPTER 4
Systems of Linear Equations; Matrices — 25
CHAPTER 5
Linear Inequalities and Linear Programming — 36
CHAPTER 6
Linear Programming: Simplex Method — 42
CHAPTER 7
Logic, Sets, and Counting — 49
CHAPTER 8
Probability — 57
CHAPTER 9
Markov Chains — 65
CHAPTER 10
Limits and the Derivative — 70
CHAPTER 11
Additional Derivative Topics — 80
CHAPTER 12
Graphing and Optimization — 86
CHAPTER 13
Integration — 95
CHAPTER 14
Additional Integration Topics — 105
CHAPTER 15
Multivariable Calculus — 111
ANSWER KEY — 121

TO THE STUDENT

COMPREHENSIVE

The *MznLnx* Exam Prep series is designed to help you pass your exams. Editors at MznLnx review your textbooks and then prepare these practice exams to help you master the textbook material. Unlike study guides, workbooks, and practice tests provided by the texbook publisher and textbook authors, *MznLnx* gives you **all** of the material in each chapter in exam form, not just samples, so you can be sure to nail your exam.

MECHANICAL

The MznLnx Exam Prep series creates exams that will help you learn the subject matter as well as test you on your understanding. Each question is designed to help you master the concept. Just working through the exams, you gain an understanding of the subject--its a simple mechanical process that produces success.

INTEGRATED STUDY GUIDE AND REVIEW

MznLnx is not just a set of exams designed to test you, its also a comprehensive review of the subject content. Each exam question is also a review of the concept, making sure that you will get the answer correct without having to go to other sources of material. You learn as you go! Its the easiest way to pass an exam.

HUMOR

Studying can be tedious and dry. MznLnx's instructional design includes moderate humor within the exam questions on occassion, to break the tedium and revitalize the brain

Chapter 1. Linear Equations and Graphs

1. The function $\log_b(x)$ depends on both b and x, but the term _____ (or logarithmic function) in standard usage refers to a function of the form $\log_b(x)$ in which the base b is fixed and so the only argument is x. Thus there is one _____ for each value of the base b (which must be positive and must differ from 1.) Viewed in this way, the base-b _____ is the inverse function of the exponential function b^x.

   a. 2-3 heap
   b. 1-center problem
   c. 120-cell
   d. Logarithm function

2. In mathematics and computer science, _____ (also base-16, hexa or base, of 16. It uses sixteen distinct symbols, most often the symbols 0-9 to represent values zero to nine, and A, B, C, D, E, F (or a through f) to represent values ten to fifteen.

   Its primary use is as a human friendly representation of binary coded values, so it is often used in digital electronics and computer engineering.

   a. Tetradecimal
   b. Factoradic
   c. Radix
   d. Hexadecimal

3. The mathematical concept of a _____ expresses the intuitive idea of deterministic dependence between two quantities, one of which is viewed as primary and the other as secondary. A _____ then is a way to associate a unique output for each input of a specified type, for example, a real number or an element of a given set.

   a. Coherent
   b. Function
   c. Going up
   d. Grill

4. In the study of metric spaces in mathematics, there are various notions of two metrics on the same underlying space being 'the same', or _____.

   In the following, M will denote a non-empty set and d_1 and d_2 will denote two metrics on M.

   The two metrics d_1 and d_2 are said to be topologically _____ if they generate the same topology on M.

   a. A posteriori
   b. Equivalent
   c. A Mathematical Theory of Communication
   d. A chemical equation

5. A _____ is an algebraic equation in which each term is either a constant or the product of a constant and a single variable. _____s can have one, two, three or more variables.

   _____s occur with great regularity in applied mathematics.

   a. Quartic equation
   b. Difference of two squares
   c. Quadratic equation
   d. Linear equation

6. In mathematics a _____ is an inequality which involves a linear function.

When operating in terms of real numbers, linear inequalities are the ones written in the forms

$$f(x) < b \text{ or } f(x) \leq b,$$

where f(x) is a linear functional in real numbers and b is a constant real number. Alternatively, these may be viewed as

$$g(x) < 0 \text{ or } g(x) \leq 0,$$

where g(x) is an affine function.

- a. Split-complex number
- b. Generalized singular value decomposition
- c. Levi-Civita symbol
- d. Linear inequality

7. In mathematics, _____ and undefined are used to explain whether or not expressions have meaningful, sensible, and unambiguous values. Not all branches of mathematics come to the same conclusion.

The following expressions are undefined in all contexts, but remarks in the analysis section may apply.

- a. Defined
- b. LHS
- c. Plugging in
- d. Toy model

8. In mathematics, an _____ is a statement about the relative size or order of two objects, or about whether they are the same or not

- The notation a < b means that a is less than b.
- The notation a > b means that a is greater than b.
- The notation a ≠ b means that a is not equal to b, but does not say that one is bigger than the other or even that they can be compared in size.

In all these cases, a is not equal to b, hence, '_____'.

These relations are known as strict _____

- The notation a ≤ b means that a is less than or equal to b;
- The notation a ≥ b means that a is greater than or equal to b;

An additional use of the notation is to show that one quantity is much greater than another, normally by several orders of magnitude.

- The notation a << b means that a is much less than b.
- The notation a >> b means that a is much greater than b.

If the sense of the _____ is the same for all values of the variables for which its members are defined, then the _____ is called an 'absolute' or 'unconditional' _____. If the sense of an _____ holds only for certain values of the variables involved, but is reversed or destroyed for other values of the variables, it is called a conditional _____.

An _____ may appear unsolvable because it only states whether a number is larger or smaller than another number; but it is possible to apply the same operations for equalities to inequalities. For example, to find x for the _____ 10x > 23 one would divide 23 by 10.

a. Inequality
c. A posteriori
b. A Mathematical Theory of Communication
d. A chemical equation

9. _____, also sometimes known as standard form or as exponential notation, is a way of writing numbers that accommodates values too large or small to be conveniently written in standard decimal notation. _____ has a number of useful properties and is often favored by scientists, mathematicians and engineers, who work with such numbers.

In _____, numbers are written in the form:

$$a \times 10^b$$

a. Leading zero
c. 1-center problem
b. Radix point
d. Scientific notation

10. In mathematics and in the sciences, a _____ (plural: _____e, formulæ or _____s) is a concise way of expressing information symbolically (as in a mathematical or chemical _____), or a general relationship between quantities. One of many famous _____e is Albert Einstein's E = mc² (see special relativity

In mathematics, a _____ is a key to solve an equation with variables. For example, the problem of determining the volume of a sphere is one that requires a significant amount of integral calculus to solve.

a. Formula
c. 1-center problem
b. 120-cell
d. 2-3 heap

11. In mathematics, a _____ is a set of real numbers with the property that any number that lies between two numbers in the set is also included in the set. For example, the set of all numbers x satisfying $0 \leq x \leq 1$ is an _____ which contains 0 and 1, as well as all numbers between them. Other examples of _____s are the set of all real numbers $\mathbb{R}$, the set of all positive real numbers, and the empty set.

a. Interval
c. Order
b. Ideal
d. Annihilator

12. _____ is the notation in which permitted values for a variable are expressed as ranging over a certain interval; "5 < x < 9" is an example of the application of _____.

a. Infinity
b. Interval notation
c. Implicit differentiation
d. A Mathematical Theory of Communication

13. In a graph theory, the _____ L

One of the earliest and most important theorems about _____s is due to Hassler Whitney, who proved that with one exceptional case the structure of G can be recovered completely from its _____.

a. Vertex-transitive graph
b. Bivariegated graph
c. Sparse graph
d. Line graph

14. In mathematics, especially in the area of abstract algebra known as combinatorial group theory, the _____ for a recursively presented group G is the algorithmic problem of deciding whether two words represent the same element. Although it is common to speak of the _____ for the group G strictly speaking it is a presentation of the group that does or does not have solvable _____. Given two finite presentations P and Q of a group G, P has solvable _____ if and only if Q does.

a. Torsion
b. Computational mathematics
c. Prime ideal theorem
d. Word problem

15. In economics, business, retail, and accounting, a _____ is the value of money that has been used up to produce something, and hence is not available for use anymore. In business, the _____ may be one of acquisition, in which case the amount of money expended to acquire it is counted as _____. In this case, money is the input that is gone in order to acquire the thing.

a. 1-center problem
b. 120-cell
c. 2-3 heap
d. Cost

16. The x-axis is the horizontal axis of a two- dimensional plot in the _____, that is typically pointed to the right. Also known as a right-handed coordinate system.

a. Cartesian coordinate system
b. 1-center problem
c. 2-3 heap
d. 120-cell

17. In mathematics, the _____ is an approach to finding a particular solution to certain inhomogeneous ordinary differential equations and recurrence relations. It is closely related to the annihilator method, but instead of using a particular kind of differential operator in order to find the best possible form of the particular solution, a 'guess' is made as to the appropriate form, which is then tested by differentiating the resulting equation. In this sense, the _____ is less formal but more intuitive than the annihilator method.

a. Linear differential equation
b. Method of undetermined coefficients
c. Differential algebraic equations
d. Phase line

18. _____ is the study of geometry using the principles of algebra. That the algebra of the real numbers can be employed to yield results about the linear continuum of geometry relies on the Cantor-Dedekind axiom. Usually the Cartesian coordinate system is applied to manipulate equations for planes, straight lines, and squares, often in two and sometimes in three dimensions of measurement.

a. Angular eccentricity
b. Analytic geometry
c. Ambient space
d. Axis-aligned object

19. In mathematics, the _____ of a Euclidean space is a special point, usually denoted by the letter O, used as a fixed point of reference for the geometry of the surrounding space. In a Cartesian coordinate system, the _____ is the point where the axes of the system intersect. In Euclidean geometry, the _____ may be chosen freely as any convenient point of reference.
   a. Autonomous system
   b. OMAC
   c. Interval
   d. Origin

20. A _____ consists of one quarter of the coordinate plane.
   a. 120-cell
   b. 1-center problem
   c. 2-3 heap
   d. Quadrant

21. _____ is a part of mathematics concerned with questions of size, shape, and relative position of figures and with properties of space. _____ is one of the oldest sciences. Initially a body of practical knowledge concerning lengths, areas, and volumes, in the third century BC _____ was put into an axiomatic form by Euclid, whose treatment--Euclidean _____--set a standard for many centuries to follow.
   a. 120-cell
   b. 1-center problem
   c. 2-3 heap
   d. Geometry

22. In mathematics, a _____ is a statement that can be proved on the basis of explicitly stated or previously agreed assumptions.
   a. Logical value
   b. Disjunction introduction
   c. Boolean function
   d. Theorem

23. A _____ typically refers to a class of handheld calculators that are capable of plotting graphs, solving simultaneous equations, and performing numerous other tasks with variables. Most popular _____s are also programmable, allowing the user to create customized programs, typically for scientific/engineering and education applications. Due to their large displays intended for graphing, they can also accommodate several lines of text and calculations at a time.
   a. Support vector machines
   b. Genus
   c. Bump mapping
   d. Graphing calculator

24. In linear algebra, the _____ of an n-by-n square matrix A is defined to be the sum of the elements on the main diagonal of A. wikimedia.org/math/8/2/b/82be32fa00bd97ebbc066aec3dfe72da.png">

where a_{ij} represents the entry on the ith row and jth column of A. Equivalently, the _____ of a matrix is the sum of its eigenvalues, making it an invariant with respect to a change of basis.

   a. Lattice
   b. Constructivism
   c. Blinding
   d. TRACE

25. A _____ is a device for performing mathematical calculations, distinguished from a computer by having a limited problem solving ability and an interface optimized for interactive calculation rather than programming. _____s can be hardware or software, and mechanical or electronic, and are often built into devices such as PDAs or mobile phones.

Modern electronic _____s are generally small, digital, and usually inexpensive.

a. 1-center problem
c. 120-cell
b. 2-3 heap
d. Calculator

26. _____ is used to describe the steepness, incline, gradient, or grade of a straight line. A higher _____ value indicates a steeper incline. The _____ is defined as the ratio of the 'rise' divided by the 'run' between two points on a line, or in other words, the ratio of the altitude change to the horizontal distance between any two points on the line.
   a. Point plotting
   b. Cognitively Guided Instruction
   c. Number line
   d. Slope

27. _____ is a form where m is the slope of the line and b is the y-intercept, which is the y-coordinate of the point where the line crosses the y axis. This can be seen by letting x = 0, which immediately gives y = b.
   a. Dynamical system
   b. Slope-intercept form
   c. Separable extension
   d. Commutative law

28. The _____ expresses the fact that the difference in the y coordinate between two points on a line that is, y − y1 is proportional to the difference in the x coordinate that is, x − x1. The proportionality constant is m (the slope of the line.
   a. Cobb-Douglas
   b. Rubin Causal Model
   c. Square function
   d. Point-slope form

29. _____ is an economic model describing effects on price and quantity in a market. It predicts that in a competitive market, price will function to equalize the quantity demanded by consumers, and the quantity supplied by producers, resulting in an economic equilibrium of price and quantity. The model incorporates other factors changing equilibrium as a shift of demand and/or supply.
   a. Marginal rate of substitution
   b. Cross price elasticity of demand
   c. 1-center problem
   d. Supply and demand

30. In mathematics, the point $\tilde{\mathbf{x}} \in \mathbb{R}^n$ is an _____ for the differential equation

$$\frac{d\mathbf{x}}{dt} = \mathbf{f}(t, \mathbf{x})$$

if $\mathbf{f}(t, \tilde{\mathbf{x}}) = 0$ for all t.

Similarly, the point $\tilde{\mathbf{x}} \in \mathbb{R}^n$ is an _____ for the difference equation

$$\mathbf{x}_{k+1} = \mathbf{f}(k, \mathbf{x}_k)$$

if $\mathbf{f}(k, \tilde{\mathbf{x}}) = \tilde{\mathbf{x}}$ for $k = 0, 1, 2, \ldots$.

Equilibria can be classified by looking at the signs of the eigenvalues of the linearization of the equations about the equilibria.

a. Equilibrium point
b. Unitary transformation
c. Algorithm design
d. Uniform algebra

31. In statistics, _____ is a form of regression analysis in which the relationship between one or more independent variables and another variable, called dependent variable, is modeled by a least squares function, called _____ equation. This function is a linear combination of one or more model parameters, called regression coefficients. A _____ equation with one independent variable represents a straight line.
    a. Random variables
    b. Percentile rank
    c. Kurtosis
    d. Linear regression

32. A _____ is an abstract model that uses mathematical language to describe the behavior of a system. Eykhoff defined a _____ as 'a representation of the essential aspects of an existing system which presents knowledge of that system in usable form'.
    a. Metaheuristic
    b. Total least squares
    c. Mathematical model
    d. Rata Die

33. The _____ fallacy is an informal fallacy. It ascribes cause where none exists. The flaw is failing to account for natural fluctuations.
    a. Depth
    b. Degrees of freedom
    c. Differential
    d. Regression

34. In mathematics, an _____, or central tendency of a data set refers to a measure of the 'middle' or 'expected' value of the data set. There are many different descriptive statistics that can be chosen as a measurement of the central tendency of the data items.

An _____ is a single value that is meant to typify a list of values.

    a. A Mathematical Theory of Communication
    b. A chemical equation
    c. A posteriori
    d. Average

35. In mathematics, the idea of _____ has come to stand for a very general idea, extending the intuitive idea of 'gluing' in topology. Since the topologists' glue is actually the use of equivalence relations on topological spaces, the theory starts with some ideas on identification.

A sophisticated theory resulted.

    a. Descent
    b. Deviance
    c. Block size
    d. Dominance

36. In mathematics, the concept of a _____ tries to capture the intuitive idea of a geometrical one-dimensional and continuous object. A simple example is the circle. In everyday use of the term '_____', a straight line is not curved, but in mathematical parlance _____s include straight lines and line segments.
    a. Negative pedal curve
    b. Curve
    c. Quadrifolium
    d. Kappa curve

Chapter 1. Linear Equations and Graphs

37. _____ is finding a curve which has the best fit to a series of data points and possibly other constraints. This section is an introduction to both interpolation and regression analysis. Both are sometimes used for extrapolation.
   a. Curve fitting
   b. Multiphysics
   c. Spectral methods
   d. Numerical stability

38. In statistics, _____ is a collective name for techniques for the modeling and analysis of numerical data consisting of values of a dependent variable and of one or more independent variables. The dependent variable in the regression equation is modeled as a function of the independent variables, corresponding parameters, and an error term. The error term is treated as a random variable.
   a. Regression analysis
   b. 1-center problem
   c. 2-3 heap
   d. 120-cell

39. A _____ is a type of display using Cartesian coordinates to display values for two variables for a set of data. The data is displayed as a collection of points, each having the value of one variable determining the position on the horizontal axis and the value of the other variable determining the position on the vertical axis. A _____ is also called a scatter chart, scatter diagram and scatter graph.
   a. 2-3 heap
   b. 1-center problem
   c. 120-cell
   d. Scatter plot

40. A _____ is is a graphical technique for presenting a data set drawn by hand or produced by a mechanical or electronic plotter. It is a graph depicting the relationship between two or more variables used, for instance, in visualising scientific data.

   _____s play an important role in statistics and data analysis.

   a. Plot
   b. Lattice
   c. Dini
   d. C-35

41. _____ is a method of constructing new data points from a discrete set of known data points.
   a. Uniform convergence
   b. Integration by substitution
   c. Interpolation
   d. Archimedes' use of infinitesimals

42. _____ is the measurement of vertical distance, but has two meanings in common use. It can either indicate how 'tall' something is, or how 'high up' it is. For example one could say 'That is a tall building', or 'That airplane is high up in the sky'.
   a. Height
   b. 2-3 heap
   c. 1-center problem
   d. 120-cell

43. In set theory, a _____ is a partially ordered set such that for each $t \in T$, the set $\{s \in T : s < t\}$ is well-ordered by the relation <. For each $t \in T$, the order type of $\{s \in T : s < t\}$ is called the height of t. The height of T itself is the least ordinal greater than the height of each element of T.
   a. Transitive reduction
   b. Definable numbers
   c. Set-theoretic topology
   d. Tree

Chapter 2. Functions and Graphs

1. The mathematical concept of a _____ expresses the intuitive idea of deterministic dependence between two quantities, one of which is viewed as primary and the other as secondary. A _____ then is a way to associate a unique output for each input of a specified type, for example, a real number or an element of a given set.
   - a. Coherent
   - b. Function
   - c. Going up
   - d. Grill

2. In mathematics, _____ and undefined are used to explain whether or not expressions have meaningful, sensible, and unambiguous values. Not all branches of mathematics come to the same conclusion.

   The following expressions are undefined in all contexts, but remarks in the analysis section may apply.
   - a. Toy model
   - b. Plugging in
   - c. Defined
   - d. LHS

3. _____ and independent variables refer to values that change in relationship to each other. The _____ are those that are observed to change in response to the independent variables. The independent variables are those that are deliberately manipulated to invoke a change in the _____.
   - a. Round robin test
   - b. Yates analysis
   - c. Steiner system
   - d. Dependent variables

4. Dependent variables and _____ refer to values that change in relationship to each other. The dependent variables are those that are observed to change in response to the _____. The _____ are those that are deliberately manipulated to invoke a change in the dependent variables.
   - a. Experimental design diagram
   - b. One-factor-at-a-time method
   - c. Operational confound
   - d. Independent variables

5. In mathematics, especially in the area of abstract algebra known as ring theory, a _____ is a ring with 0 ≠ 1 such that ab = 0 implies that either a = 0 or b = 0. That is, it is a nontrivial ring without left or right zero divisors. A commutative _____ is called an integral _____.
   - a. Modular representation theory
   - b. Simple ring
   - c. Left primitive ring
   - d. Domain

6. In mathematics, a _____ is a function whose values do not vary and thus are constant. For example, if we have the function f→ B is a _____ iff f
   - a. Point reflection
   - b. Constant Function
   - c. Linear operator
   - d. Squeeze mapping

7. In mathematics, a _____ is the end result of a division problem. It can also be expressed as the number of times the divisor divides into the dividend.
   - a. Limiting
   - b. Marginal cost
   - c. Notation
   - d. Quotient

8. In economics, business, retail, and accounting, a _____ is the value of money that has been used up to produce something, and hence is not available for use anymore. In business, the _____ may be one of acquisition, in which case the amount of money expended to acquire it is counted as _____. In this case, money is the input that is gone in order to acquire the thing.

a. 1-center problem
b. 120-cell
c. 2-3 heap
d. Cost

9. In economics, the cross elasticity of demand and _____ measures the responsiveness of the quantity demanded of a good to a change in the price of another good.

It is measured as the percentage change in quantity demanded for the first good that occurs in response to a percentage change in price of the second good. For example, if, in response to a 10% increase in the price of fuel, the quantity of new cars that are fuel inefficient demanded decreased by 20%, the cross elasticity of demand would be -20%/10% = -2.

a. Marginal rate of substitution
b. Supply and demand
c. Cross price elasticity of demand
d. 1-center problem

10. A _____ is an abstract model that uses mathematical language to describe the behavior of a system. Eykhoff defined a _____ as 'a representation of the essential aspects of an existing system which presents knowledge of that system in usable form'.

a. Rata Die
b. Total least squares
c. Metaheuristic
d. Mathematical model

11. In computational complexity theory, the complexity class _____ is the union of the classes in the exponential hierarchy.

$$\text{ELEMENTARY} = \text{EXP} \cup \text{2EXP} \cup \text{3EXP} \cup \cdots$$
$$= \text{DTIME}(2^n) \cup \text{DTIME}(2^{2^n}) \cup \text{DTIME}(2^{2^{2^n}}) \cup \cdots$$

The name was coined by Laszlo Kalmar, in the context of recursive functions and undecidability; most problems in it are far from _____. Some natural recursive problems lie outside _____, and are thus NONELEMENTARY.

a. A chemical equation
b. A Mathematical Theory of Communication
c. A posteriori
d. Elementary

12. In mathematics, an _____ is a function built from a finite number of exponentials, logarithms, constants, one variable, and roots of equations through composition and combinations using the four elementary operations (+ - × ÷.) The trigonometric functions and their inverses are assumed to be included in the _____s by using complex variables and the relations between the trigonometric functions and the exponential and logarithm functions.

_____s are considered a subset of special functions.

a. A posteriori
b. Elementary function
c. A Mathematical Theory of Communication
d. A chemical equation

13. In mathematics, the _____ of a real number is its numerical value without regard to its sign. So, for example, 3 is the _____ of both 3 and −3.

Chapter 2. Functions and Graphs   11

The _____ of a number a is denoted by $|a|$.

Generalizations of the _____ for real numbers occur in a wide variety of mathematical settings.

a. Area hyperbolic functions
b. A Mathematical Theory of Communication
c. A chemical equation
d. Absolute value

14. A _____ of a number is a number a such that $a^3 = x$.
    a. Golden function
    b. Square root
    c. Hyperbolic functions
    d. Cube root

15. In mathematics, the term _____ has several different important meanings:

    - An _____ is an equality that remains true regardless of the values of any variables that appear within it, to distinguish it from an equality which is true under more particular conditions. For this, the 'triple bar' symbol ≡ is sometimes used.
    - In algebra, an _____ or _____ element of a set S with a binary operation Â· is an element e that, when combined with any element x of S, produces that same x. That is, eÂ·x = xÂ·e = x for all x in S.
        o The _____ function from a set S to itself, often denoted id or id$_s$, s the function such that i = x for all x in S. This function serves as the _____ element in the set of all functions from S to itself with respect to function composition.
        o In linear algebra, the _____ matrix of size n is the n-by-n square matrix with ones on the main diagonal and zeros elsewhere. This matrix serves as the _____ with respect to matrix multiplication.

A common example of the first meaning is the trigonometric _____

$$\sin^2 \theta + \cos^2 \theta = 1$$

which is true for all real values of θ, as opposed to

$$\cos \theta = 1,$$

which is true only for some values of θ, not all. For example, the latter equation is true when $\theta = 0$, false when $\theta = 2$

The concepts of 'additive _____' and 'multiplicative _____' are central to the Peano axioms. The number 0 is the 'additive _____' for integers, real numbers, and complex numbers. For the real numbers, for all $a \in \mathbb{R}$,

$$0 + a = a,$$

$$a + 0 = a, \text{ and}$$

$$0 + 0 = 0.$$

Similarly, The number 1 is the 'multiplicative _____' for integers, real numbers, and complex numbers.

a. Action
b. Intersection
c. ARIA
d. Identity

16. An _____ is a function that does not have any effect: it always returns the same value that was used as its argument.
a. Inverse function
b. Angle bisector
c. Algebra
d. Identity function

17. In descriptive statistics, the _____ is the length of the smallest interval which contains all the data. It is calculated by subtracting the smallest observations from the greatest and provides an indication of statistical dispersion.

It is measured in the same units as the data.

a. Kernel
b. Range
c. Class
d. Bandwidth

18. In mathematics, a _____ is a square root of a function with respect to the operation of function composition. In other words, the functional square root of a function g is a function f satisfying f(f(x)) = g(x) for all x. For example, f(x) = 2x2 is a functional square root of g(x) = 8x4.
a. Total least squares
b. Debt
c. Point-slope form
d. Square function

19. In mathematics, a _____ of a number x is a number r such that r^2 = x, or, in other words, a number r whose square is x. Every non-negative real number x has a unique non-negative _____, called the principal _____, which is denoted with a radical symbol as $\sqrt{x}$, or, using exponent notation, as $x^{1/2}$. For example, the principal _____ of 9 is 3, denoted $\sqrt{9}$ = 3, because 3^2 = 3 × 3 = 9.
a. Hyperbolic functions
b. Double exponential
c. Square root
d. Multiplicative inverse

Chapter 2. Functions and Graphs

20. In vascular plants, the _____ is the organ of a plant body that typically lies below the surface of the soil. This is not always the case, however, since a _____ can also be aerial (that is, growing above the ground) or aerating (that is, growing up above the ground or especially above water.) Furthermore, a stem normally occurring below ground is not exceptional either

   a. 1-center problem
   b. Root
   c. 120-cell
   d. 2-3 heap

21. In mathematics, a _____ is a function whose definition is dependent on the value of the independent variable. Mathematically, a real-valued function f of a real variable x is a relationship whose definition is given differently on disjoint subsets of its domain

The word piecewise is also used to describe any property of a _____ that holds for each piece but may not hold for the whole domain of the function.

   a. Surjective
   b. High-dimensional model representation
   c. Piecewise-defined Function
   d. Glide reflection

22. In mathematics, the _____ is a conic section, the intersection of a right circular conical surface and a plane parallel to a generating straight line of that surface. Given a point and a line that lie in a plane, the locus of points in that plane that are equidistant to them is a _____.

A particular case arises when the plane is tangent to the conical surface of a circle.

   a. Parabola
   b. Matrix representation of conic sections
   c. Directrix
   d. Dandelin sphere

23. A _____, in mathematics, is a polynomial function of the form $f(x) = ax^2 + bx + c$, where $a \neq 0$. The graph of a _____ is a parabola whose major axis is parallel to the y-axis.

The expression $ax^2 + bx + c$ in the definition of a _____ is a polynomial of degree 2 or a 2nd degree polynomial, because the highest exponent of x is 2.

   a. Laguerre polynomials
   b. Multivariate division algorithm
   c. Quadratic function
   d. Discriminant

24. In mathematics, an _____ is a statement about the relative size or order of two objects, or about whether they are the same or not

   - The notation a < b means that a is less than b.
   - The notation a > b means that a is greater than b.
   - The notation a ≠ b means that a is not equal to b, but does not say that one is bigger than the other or even that they can be compared in size.

In all these cases, a is not equal to b, hence, '_____'.

These relations are known as strict _____

- The notation a ≤ b means that a is less than or equal to b;
- The notation a ≥ b means that a is greater than or equal to b;

An additional use of the notation is to show that one quantity is much greater than another, normally by several orders of magnitude.

- The notation a << b means that a is much less than b.
- The notation a >> b means that a is much greater than b.

If the sense of the _____ is the same for all values of the variables for which its members are defined, then the _____ is called an 'absolute' or 'unconditional' _____. If the sense of an _____ holds only for certain values of the variables involved, but is reversed or destroyed for other values of the variables, it is called a conditional _____.

An _____ may appear unsolvable because it only states whether a number is larger or smaller than another number; but it is possible to apply the same operations for equalities to inequalities. For example, to find x for the _____ 10x > 23 one would divide 23 by 10.

a. A Mathematical Theory of Communication
b. A posteriori
c. A chemical equation
d. Inequality

25. _____, also sometimes known as standard form or as exponential notation, is a way of writing numbers that accommodates values too large or small to be conveniently written in standard decimal notation. _____ has a number of useful properties and is often favored by scientists, mathematicians and engineers, who work with such numbers.

In _____, numbers are written in the form:

$$a \times 10^b$$

a. Leading zero
b. Radix point
c. 1-center problem
d. Scientific notation

26. In geometry, a _____ is a special kind of point, usually a corner of a polygon, polyhedron, or higher dimensional polytope. In the geometry of curves a _____ is a point of where the first derivative of curvature is zero. In graph theory, a _____ is the fundamental unit out of which graphs are formed

a. Dini
b. Crib
c. Duality
d. Vertex

27. In mathematics, a _____ is an expression constructed from variables and constants, using the operations of addition, subtraction, multiplication, and constant non-negative whole number exponents. For example, $x^2 - 4x + 7$ is a _____, but $x^2 - 4/x + 7x^{3/2}$ is not, because its second term involves division by the variable x and also because its third term contains an exponent that is not a whole number.

_____s are one of the most important concepts in algebra and throughout mathematics and science.

a. Group extension
b. Coimage
c. Polynomial
d. Semifield

28. In mathematics, a _____ is any function which can be written as the ratio of two polynomial functions. _____ of degree 2 :

$$y = \frac{x^2 - 3x - 2}{x^2 - 4}$$

In the case of one variable, x, a _____ is a function of the form

$$f(x) = \frac{P(x)}{Q(x)}$$

where P and Q are polynomial function in x and Q is not the zero polynomial. The domain of f is the set of all points x for which the denominator Q

a. Legendre rational functions
b. Rational function
c. 1-center problem
d. 120-cell

29. In probability theory, a probability distribution is called _____ if its cumulative distribution function is _____. That is equivalent to saying that for random variables X with the distribution in question, Pr[X = a] = 0 for all real numbers a. If the distribution of X is _____ then X is called a _____ random variable.

a. Conull set
b. Concatenated codes
c. Continuous phase modulation
d. Continuous

30. Suppose f is a function. Then the line y = a is a _____ for f if

$$\lim_{x \to \infty} f(x) = a \text{ or } \lim_{x \to -\infty} f(x) = a.$$

Intuitively, this means that f(x) can be made as close as desired to a by making x big enough. How big is big enough depends on how close one wishes to make f(x) to a.

a. 120-cell
b. 1-center problem
c. 2-3 heap
d. Horizontal asymptote

31. An _____ of a real-valued function y = f(x) is a curve which describes the behavior of f as either x or y tends to infinity.

In other words, as one moves along the graph of f(x) in some direction, the distance between it and the _____ eventually becomes smaller than any distance that one may specify.

If a curve A has the curve B as an _____, one says that A is asymptotic to B. Similarly B is asymptotic to A, so A and B are called asymptotic.

a. Infinite product
c. Improper integral

b. Isoperimetric dimension
d. Asymptote

32. The _____ is a function in mathematics. The application of this function to a value x is written as ex. Equivalently, this can be written in the form e^x, where e is a mathematical constant, the base of the natural logarithm, which equals approximately 2.718281828, and is also known as Euler's number.

a. Area hyperbolic functions
c. Exponential function

b. A chemical equation
d. A Mathematical Theory of Communication

33. In mathematics and computer science, _____ (also base-16, hexa or base, of 16. It uses sixteen distinct symbols, most often the symbols 0-9 to represent values zero to nine, and A, B, C, D, E, F (or a through f) to represent values ten to fifteen.

Its primary use is as a human friendly representation of binary coded values, so it is often used in digital electronics and computer engineering.

a. Tetradecimal
c. Hexadecimal

b. Factoradic
d. Radix

34. A _____ is a software program that facilitates symbolic mathematics. The core functionality of a CAS is manipulation of mathematical expressions in symbolic form.

Chapter 2. Functions and Graphs

The symbolic manipulations supported typically include

- simplification to the smallest possible expression or some standard form, including automatic simplification with assumptions and simplification with constraints
- substitution of symbolic, functors or numeric values for expressions
- change of form of expressions: expanding products and powers, partial and full factorization, rewriting as partial fractions, constraint satisfaction, rewriting trigonometric functions as exponentials, etc.
- partial and total differentiation
- symbolic constrained and unconstrained global optimization
- solution of linear and some non-linear equations over various domains
- solution of some differential and difference equations
- taking some limits
- some indefinite and definite integration, including multidimensional integrals
- integral transforms
- arbitrary-precision numeric operations
- Series operations such as expansion, summation and products
- matrix operations including products, inverses, etc.
- display of mathematical expressions in two-dimensional mathematical form, often using typesetting systems similar to TeX
- add-ons for use in applied mathematics such as physics packages for physical computation
- plotting graphs and parametric plots of functions in two and three dimensions, and animating them
- APIs for linking it on an external program such as a database, or using in a programming language to use the _____
- drawing charts and diagrams
- string manipulation such as matching and searching
- statistical computation
- Theorem proving and verification
- graphic production and editing such as CGI and signal processing as image processing
- sound synthesis

Many also include a programming language, allowing users to implement their own algorithms.

Some _____ s focus on a specific area of application; these are typically developed in academia and are free.

a. 1-center problem
c. Computer algebra system
b. 120-cell
d. 2-3 heap

35. _____ occurs when the growth rate of a mathematical function is proportional to the function's current value. In the case of a discrete domain of definition with equal intervals it is also called geometric growth or geometric decay.

With _____ of a positive value its rate of increase steadily increases, or in the case of exponential decay, its rate of decrease steadily decreases.

Chapter 2. Functions and Graphs

a. A Mathematical Theory of Communication
b. A posteriori
c. A chemical equation
d. Exponential growth

36. The _____ fallacy is an informal fallacy. It ascribes cause where none exists. The flaw is failing to account for natural fluctuations.
   a. Degrees of freedom
   b. Depth
   c. Differential
   d. Regression

37. _____ is a fee, paid on borrowed capital. Assets lent include money, shares, consumer goods through hire purchase, major assets such as aircraft, and even entire factories in finance lease arrangements. The _____ is calculated upon the value of the assets in the same manner as upon money.
   a. Interest sensitivity gap
   b. A Mathematical Theory of Communication
   c. Interest expense
   d. Interest

38. _____ is the concept of adding accumulated interest back to the principal, so that interest is earned on interest from that moment on. The act of declaring interest to be principal is called compounding. A loan, for example, may have its interest compounded every month: in this case, a loan with $100 principal and 1% interest per month would have a balance of $101 at the end of the first month.
   a. Net interest margin
   b. Compound interest
   c. Retained interest
   d. Net interest margin securities

39. The function $\log_b(x)$ depends on both b and x, but the term _____ (or logarithmic function) in standard usage refers to a function of the form $\log_b(x)$ in which the base b is fixed and so the only argument is x. Thus there is one _____ for each value of the base b (which must be positive and must differ from 1.) Viewed in this way, the base-b _____ is the inverse function of the exponential function b^x.
   a. 120-cell
   b. 1-center problem
   c. 2-3 heap
   d. Logarithm function

40. In mathematics, the _____ of a number n is the number that, when added to n, yields zero. The _____ of n is denoted −n. For example, 7 is −7, because 7 + (−7) = 0, and the _____ of −0.3 is 0.3, because −0.3 + 0.3 = 0.
   a. Associativity
   b. Additive inverse
   c. Algebraic structure
   d. Arity

41. An _____ is a function which does the reverse of a given function.
   a. A Mathematical Theory of Communication
   b. Empty set
   c. Empty function
   d. Inverse function

42. An injective function is called an injection, and is also said to be a _____ (not to be confused with one-to-one correspondence, i.e. a bijective function.)

A function f that is not injective is sometimes called many-to-one. (However, this terminology is also sometimes used to mean 'single-valued', i.e. each argument is mapped to at most one value.)

   a. A posteriori
   b. A chemical equation
   c. A Mathematical Theory of Communication
   d. One-to-one function

Chapter 2. Functions and Graphs

43. In mathematics, the _____ of a number to a given base is the power or exponent to which the base must be raised in order to produce the number.

For example, the _____ of 1000 to the base 10 is 3, because 3 is how many 10s one must multiply to get 1000: thus 10 × 10 × 10 = 1000; the base-2 _____ of 32 is 5 because 5 is how many 2s one must multiply to get 32: thus 2 × 2 × 2 × 2 × 2 = 32. In the language of exponents: 10^3 = 1000, so $\log_{10} 1000$ = 3, and 2^5 = 32, so $\log_2 32$ = 5.

a. 2-3 heap
b. Logarithm
c. 1-center problem
d. 120-cell

44. The _____, formerly known as the hyperbolic logarithm, is the logarithm to the base e, where e is an irrational constant approximately equal to 2.718 281 828. It is also sometimes referred to as the Napierian logarithm, although the original meaning of this term is slightly different. In simple terms, the _____ of a number x is the power to which e would have to be raised to equal x -- for example the natural log of e itself is 1 because e^1 = e, while the _____ of 1 would be 0, since e^0 = 1.

a. 1-center problem
b. Logarithmic identities
c. Logarithmic growth
d. Natural logarithm

45. A _____ is a device for performing mathematical calculations, distinguished from a computer by having a limited problem solving ability and an interface optimized for interactive calculation rather than programming. _____s can be hardware or software, and mechanical or electronic, and are often built into devices such as PDAs or mobile phones.

Modern electronic _____s are generally small, digital, and usually inexpensive.

a. 120-cell
b. 2-3 heap
c. 1-center problem
d. Calculator

46. The _____ is the period of time required for a quantity to double in size or value.

a. Zenzizenzizenzic
b. Power law
c. Stretched exponential function
d. Doubling time

47. In computational complexity theory, an algorithm is said to take _____ if the asymptotic upper bound for the time it requires is proportional to the size of the input, which is usually denoted n.

Informally spoken, the running time increases linearly with the size of the input. For example, a procedure that adds up all elements of a list requires time proportional to the length of the list.

a. Truth table reduction
b. Constructible function
c. Time-constructible function
d. Linear time

Chapter 3. Mathematics of Finance

1. In abstract algebra, a module S over a ring R is called _____ or irreducible if it is not the zero module 0 and if its only submodules are 0 and S. Understanding the _____ modules over a ring is usually helpful because these modules form the 'building blocks' of all other modules in a certain sense.

Abelian groups are the same as Z-modules.

- a. Basis
- b. Harmonic series
- c. Simple
- d. Derivation

2. In mathematics, _____ and undefined are used to explain whether or not expressions have meaningful, sensible, and unambiguous values. Not all branches of mathematics come to the same conclusion.

The following expressions are undefined in all contexts, but remarks in the analysis section may apply.

- a. LHS
- b. Plugging in
- c. Toy model
- d. Defined

3. In mathematics and in the sciences, a _____ (plural: _____e, formulæ or _____s) is a concise way of expressing information symbolically (as in a mathematical or chemical _____), or a general relationship between quantities. One of many famous _____e is Albert Einstein's $E = mc^2$ (see special relativity

In mathematics, a _____ is a key to solve an equation with variables. For example, the problem of determining the volume of a sphere is one that requires a significant amount of integral calculus to solve.

- a. Formula
- b. 1-center problem
- c. 2-3 heap
- d. 120-cell

4. _____ is a fee, paid on borrowed capital. Assets lent include money, shares, consumer goods through hire purchase, major assets such as aircraft, and even entire factories in finance lease arrangements. The _____ is calculated upon the value of the assets in the same manner as upon money.

- a. Interest
- b. Interest expense
- c. A Mathematical Theory of Communication
- d. Interest sensitivity gap

5. In mathematics, hyperbolic n-space, denoted H^n, is the maximally symmetric, simply connected, n-dimensional Riemannian manifold with constant sectional curvature −1. _____ is the principal example of a space exhibiting hyperbolic geometry. It can be thought of as the negative-curvature analogue of the n-sphere.

- a. Horocycle
- b. Hyperbolic geometry
- c. Hyperbolic space
- d. Margulis lemma

6. _____ is the concept of adding accumulated interest back to the principal, so that interest is earned on interest from that moment on. The act of declaring interest to be principal is called compounding. A loan, for example, may have its interest compounded every month: in this case, a loan with $100 principal and 1% interest per month would have a balance of $101 at the end of the first month.

- a. Retained interest
- b. Compound interest
- c. Net interest margin securities
- d. Net interest margin

Chapter 3. Mathematics of Finance

7. In probability theory, a probability distribution is called _____ if its cumulative distribution function is _____. That is equivalent to saying that for random variables X with the distribution in question, Pr[X = a] = 0 for all real numbers a. If the distribution of X is _____ then X is called a _____ random variable.
   - a. Continuous phase modulation
   - b. Conull set
   - c. Continuous
   - d. Concatenated codes

8. In mathematics, a _____ is a number that can be expressed as an integral of an algebraic function over an algebraic domain. Kontsevich and Zagier define a _____ as a complex number whose real and imaginary parts are values of absolutely convergent integrals of rational functions with rational coefficients, over domains in given by polynomial inequalities with rational coefficients.
   - a. Disk
   - b. Closeness
   - c. Boussinesq approximation
   - d. Period

9. A _____ typically refers to a class of handheld calculators that are capable of plotting graphs, solving simultaneous equations, and performing numerous other tasks with variables. Most popular _____s are also programmable, allowing the user to create customized programs, typically for scientific/engineering and education applications. Due to their large displays intended for graphing, they can also accommodate several lines of text and calculations at a time.
   - a. Genus
   - b. Support vector machines
   - c. Graphing calculator
   - d. Bump mapping

10. A _____ is a device for performing mathematical calculations, distinguished from a computer by having a limited problem solving ability and an interface optimized for interactive calculation rather than programming. _____s can be hardware or software, and mechanical or electronic, and are often built into devices such as PDAs or mobile phones.

    Modern electronic _____s are generally small, digital, and usually inexpensive.

    - a. 2-3 heap
    - b. 120-cell
    - c. 1-center problem
    - d. Calculator

11. _____ is usually defined as the activity of using and developing computer technology, computer hardware and software. It is the computer-specific part of information technology. Computer science (or _____ science) is the study and the science of the theoretical foundations of information and computation and their implementation and application in computer systems.
    - a. Parallel Random Access Machine
    - b. Probabilistic Turing Machine
    - c. Deterministic finite state machine
    - d. Computing

12. In computational complexity theory, an algorithm is said to take _____ if the asymptotic upper bound for the time it requires is proportional to the size of the input, which is usually denoted n.

    Informally spoken, the running time increases linearly with the size of the input. For example, a procedure that adds up all elements of a list requires time proportional to the length of the list.

    - a. Constructible function
    - b. Truth table reduction
    - c. Time-constructible function
    - d. Linear time

Chapter 3. Mathematics of Finance

13. _____ expresses an annual rate of interest taking into account the effect of compounding, usually for deposit or investment products. It is analogous to the Annual percentage rate, which is used for loans. In some jurisdictions, the use and definition of _____ may be regulated by a government agency, in which case it would generally be capitalized.
   a. Annual percentage yield
   b. A Mathematical Theory of Communication
   c. A posteriori
   d. A chemical equation

14. In mathematics, a _____ is a way of expressing a number as a fraction of 100. It is often denoted using the percent sign, '%'. For example, 45% is equal to 45 / 100, or 0.45.
   a. Subtrahend
   b. Least common multiple
   c. Lowest common denominator
   d. Percentage

15. The term _____ refers to the central sense organ complex, for those animals that have one, normally on the ventral surface of the head and can depending on the definition in the human case, include the hair, forehead, eyebrow, eyes, nose, ears, cheeks, mouth, lips, philtrum, teeth, skin, and chin. The _____ has uses of expression, appearance, and identity amongst others.It also has different senses like smelling, tasting, hearing, and seeing.

Caricatures often exaggerate facial features to make a _____ more easily recognized in association with a pronounced portion of the _____ of the individual in question--for example, a caricature of Osama bin Laden might focus on his facial hair and nose; a caricature of George W. Bush might enlarge his ears to the size of an elephant¢s; a caricature of Jay Leno may pronounce his head and chin; and a caricature of Mick Jagger might enlarge his lips.

   a. 2-3 heap
   b. 1-center problem
   c. 120-cell
   d. Face

16. In mathematics, especially in the area of abstract algebra known as combinatorial group theory, the _____ for a recursively presented group G is the algorithmic problem of deciding whether two words represent the same element. Although it is common to speak of the _____ for the group G strictly speaking it is a presentation of the group that does or does not have solvable _____. Given two finite presentations P and Q of a group G, P has solvable _____ if and only if Q does.
   a. Computational mathematics
   b. Prime ideal theorem
   c. Torsion
   d. Word problem

17. In quantum field theory and statistical mechanics in the thermodynamic limit, a system with a global symmetry can have more than one phase. For parameters where the symmetry is spontaneously broken, the system is said to be _____. When the global symmetry is unbroken the system is disordered.
   a. Isoenthalpic-isobaric ensemble
   b. Einstein relation
   c. Ursell function
   d. Ordered

18. In mathematics, an _____ is a collection of objects having two coordinates (or entries or projections), such that one can always uniquely determine the object, which is the first coordinate (or first entry or left projection) of the pair as well as the second coordinate (or second entry or right projection.) If the first coordinate is a and the second is b, the usual notation for an _____ is (a, b.) The pair is 'ordered' in that (a, b) differs from (b, a) unless a = b.
   a. A Mathematical Theory of Communication
   b. A posteriori
   c. Ordered pair
   d. A chemical equation

Chapter 3. Mathematics of Finance

19. In mathematics, the _____s may be described informally in several different ways. The _____s include both rational numbers, such as 42 and −23/129, and irrational numbers, such as pi and the square root of two; or, a _____ can be given by an infinite decimal representation, such as 2.4871773339...., where the digits continue in some way; or, the _____s may be thought of as points on an infinitely long number line.

These descriptions of the _____s, while intuitively accessible, are not sufficiently rigorous for the purposes of pure mathematics.

   a. Pre-algebra
   b. Minkowski distance
   c. Tally marks
   d. Real number

20. _____ or amortisation is the process of decreasing an amount over a period of time. The word comes from Middle English amortisen to kill, alienate in mortmain, from Anglo-French amorteser, alteration of amortir, from Vulgar Latin admortire to kill, from Latin ad- + mort-, mors death. Particular instances of the term include:

   - _____, the allocation of a lump sum amount to different time periods, particularly for loans and other forms of finance, including related interest or other finance charges.
     - _____ schedule, a table detailing each periodic payment on a loan, as generated by an _____ calculator.
     - Negative _____, an _____ schedule where the loan amount actually increases through not paying the full interest
   - Amortized analysis, analyzing the execution cost of algorithms over a sequence of operations.
   - _____ of capital expenditures of certain assets under accounting rules, particularly intangible assets, in a manner analogous to depreciation.
   - _____

_____ is also used in the context of zoning regulations and describes the time in which a property owner has to relocate when the property's use constitutes a preexisting nonconforming use under zoning regulations.

   - Depreciation

   a. Identity
   b. Amortization
   c. Origin
   d. ISAAC

21. _____ is that which is owed; usually referencing assets owed, but the term can cover other obligations. In the case of assets, _____ is a means of using future purchasing power in the present before a summation has been earned.
   a. Point-slope form
   b. Metaheuristic
   c. Cobb-Douglas
   d. Debt

22. An _____ is a table detailing each periodic payment on a amortizing loan, as generated by an amortization calculator.

While a portion of every payment is applied towards both the interest and the principal balance of the loan, the exact amount applied to principal each time varies. An _____ reveals the specific monetary amount put towards interest, as well as the specific put towards the Principal balance, with each payment.

a. A Mathematical Theory of Communication
b. A chemical equation
c. Amortization schedule
d. Accounts receivable

23. _____ is the concept or idea of fairness in economics, particularly as to taxation or welfare economics.
a. Union
b. Interval
c. Event
d. Equity

24. _____ is the value of a homeowner's unencumbered interest in their property, i.e. the difference between the home's fair market value and the unpaid balance of the mortgage and any outstanding debt over the home. Equity increases as the mortgage is paid or as the property enjoys appreciation. This is sometimes called real property value in economics.
a. 120-cell
b. 1-center problem
c. Real estate
d. Home equity

25. In game theory, a player's _____ in a game is a complete plan of action for whatever situation might arise; this fully determines the player's behaviour. A player's _____ will determine the action the player will take at any stage of the game, for every possible history of play up to that stage.

A _____ profile is a set of strategies for each player which fully specifies all actions in a game.

a. Matching pennies
b. Correlated equilibrium
c. Sir Philip Sidney game
d. Strategy

Chapter 4. Systems of Linear Equations; Matrices

1. In linear algebra, the _____ of a matrix is obtained by changing a matrix in some way.

   Given the matrices A and B, where:

   $$A = \begin{bmatrix} 1 & 3 & 2 \\ 2 & 0 & 1 \\ 5 & 2 & 2 \end{bmatrix}, \quad B = \begin{bmatrix} 4 \\ 3 \\ 1 \end{bmatrix}$$

   Then, the _____ is written as:

   $$(A|B) = \begin{bmatrix} 1 & 3 & 2 & 4 \\ 2 & 0 & 1 & 3 \\ 5 & 2 & 2 & 1 \end{bmatrix}$$

   This is useful when solving systems of linear equations or the _____ may also be used to find the inverse of a matrix by combining it with the identity matrix.

   Let C be a square 2×2 matrix where $$C = \begin{bmatrix} 1 & 3 \\ -5 & 0 \end{bmatrix}$$

   To find the inverse of C we create where I is the 2×2 identity matrix.

   a. Augmented matrix
   c. Alternating sign matrix
   b. Unimodular polynomial matrix
   d. Eigendecomposition

2. A _____ is an algebraic equation in which each term is either a constant or the product of a constant and a single variable. _____s can have one, two, three or more variables.

   _____s occur with great regularity in applied mathematics.

   a. Difference of two squares
   c. Linear equation
   b. Quadratic equation
   d. Quartic equation

3. _____ is a branch of mathematics which focuses on the study of matrices. Initially a sub-branch of linear algebra, it has grown to cover subjects related to graph theory, algebra, combinatorics, and statistics as well.

   The term matrix was first coined in 1848 by J.J. Sylvester as a name of an array of numbers.

   a. Segre classification
   c. Pairing
   b. Semi-simple operators
   d. Matrix theory

Chapter 4. Systems of Linear Equations; Matrices

4. In mathematics, a _____ is a rectangular table of elements, which may be numbers or, more generally, any abstract quantities that can be added and multiplied. Matrices are used to describe linear equations, keep track of the coefficients of linear transformations and to record data that depend on multiple parameters. Matrices are described by the field of _____ theory.

a. Coherent
b. Double counting
c. Compression
d. Matrix

5. In logic, a theory is _____ if it does not contain a contradiction. The lack of contradiction can be defined in either semantic or syntactic terms. The semantic definition states that a theory is _____ if it has a model; this is the sense used in traditional Aristotelian logic, although in contemporary mathematical logic the term satisfiable is used instead.

a. Second-order logic
b. Logic
c. Consistent
d. First-order logic

6. In the study of metric spaces in mathematics, there are various notions of two metrics on the same underlying space being 'the same', or _____.

In the following, M will denote a non-empty set and d_1 and d_2 will denote two metrics on M.

The two metrics d_1 and d_2 are said to be topologically _____ if they generate the same topology on M.

a. A Mathematical Theory of Communication
b. A chemical equation
c. A posteriori
d. Equivalent

7. A _____ is a device for performing mathematical calculations, distinguished from a computer by having a limited problem solving ability and an interface optimized for interactive calculation rather than programming. _____s can be hardware or software, and mechanical or electronic, and are often built into devices such as PDAs or mobile phones.

Modern electronic _____s are generally small, digital, and usually inexpensive.

a. 2-3 heap
b. Calculator
c. 120-cell
d. 1-center problem

8. A _____ typically refers to a class of handheld calculators that are capable of plotting graphs, solving simultaneous equations, and performing numerous other tasks with variables. Most popular _____s are also programmable, allowing the user to create customized programs, typically for scientific/engineering and education applications. Due to their large displays intended for graphing, they can also accommodate several lines of text and calculations at a time.

a. Support vector machines
b. Genus
c. Bump mapping
d. Graphing calculator

9. In mathematics, the point $\tilde{\mathbf{x}} \in \mathbb{R}^n$ is an _____ for the differential equation

$$\frac{d\mathbf{x}}{dt} = \mathbf{f}(t, \mathbf{x})$$

if $f(t, \tilde{x}) = 0$ for all t.

Similarly, the point $\tilde{x} \in \mathbb{R}^n$ is an _____ for the difference equation

$$x_{k+1} = f(k, x_k)$$

if $f(k, \tilde{x}) = \tilde{x}$ for $k = 0, 1, 2, \ldots$.

Equilibria can be classified by looking at the signs of the eigenvalues of the linearization of the equations about the equilibria.

a. Uniform algebra
c. Algorithm design
b. Equilibrium point
d. Unitary transformation

10. In mathematics, an _____ or member of a set is any one of the distinct objects that make up that set.

Writing A = {1,2,3,4}, means that the _____s of the set A are the numbers 1, 2, 3 and 4. Groups of _____s of A, for example {1,2}, are subsets of A.

a. Ideal
c. Universal code
b. Order
d. Element

11. In linear algebra, a row vector or _____ is a 1 × n matrix, that is, a matrix consisting of a single row:

$$x = \begin{bmatrix} x_1 & x_2 & \cdots & x_m \end{bmatrix}.$$

The transpose of a row vector is a column vector:

$$\begin{bmatrix} x_1 \\ x_2 \\ \vdots \\ x_m \end{bmatrix} = \begin{bmatrix} x_1 & x_2 & \cdots & x_m \end{bmatrix}^T.$$

The set of all row vectors forms a vector space which is the dual space to the set of all column vectors.

Chapter 4. Systems of Linear Equations; Matrices

Row vectors are sometimes written using the following non-standard notation:

$$\mathbf{x} = \begin{bmatrix} x_1, x_2, \ldots, x_m \end{bmatrix}.$$

- Matrix multiplication involves the action of multiplying each row vector of one matrix by each column vector of another matrix.

- The dot product of two vectors a and b is equivalent to multiplying the row vector representation of a by the column vector representation of b:

$$\mathbf{a} \cdot \mathbf{b} = \begin{bmatrix} a_1 & a_2 & a_3 \end{bmatrix} \begin{bmatrix} b_1 \\ b_2 \\ b_3 \end{bmatrix}.$$

a. Woodbury matrix identity
c. Gram-Schmidt process
b. Dual vector space
d. Row matrix

12. In linear algebra, a column vector or _____ is an m × 1 matrix, i.e. a matrix consisting of a single column of m elements.

$$\mathbf{x} = \begin{bmatrix} x_1 \\ x_2 \\ \vdots \\ x_m \end{bmatrix}$$

The transpose of a column vector is a row vector and vice versa.

The set of all column vectors forms a vector space which is the dual space to the set of all row vectors.

a. Spread of a matrix
c. Split-complex number
b. Cayley-Hamilton theorem
d. Column matrix

13. In mathematics, _____ and undefined are used to explain whether or not expressions have meaningful, sensible, and unambiguous values. Not all branches of mathematics come to the same conclusion.

The following expressions are undefined in all contexts, but remarks in the analysis section may apply.

a. LHS
c. Toy model
b. Plugging in
d. Defined

Chapter 4. Systems of Linear Equations; Matrices

14. In mathematics, an _____ in the sense of ring theory is a subring $\mathcal{O}$ of a ring R that satisfies the conditions

    1. R is a ring which is a finite-dimensional algebra over the rational number field $\mathbb{Q}$
    2. $\mathcal{O}$ spans R over $\mathbb{Q}$, so that $\mathbb{Q}\mathcal{O} = R$, and
    3. $\mathcal{O}$ is a lattice in R.

The third condition can be stated more accurately, in terms of the extension of scalars of R to the real numbers, embedding R in a real vector space. In less formal terms, additively $\mathcal{O}$ should be a free abelian group generated by a basis for R over $\mathbb{Q}$.

The leading example is the case where R is a number field K and $\mathcal{O}$ is its ring of integers. In algebraic number theory there are examples for any K other than the rational field of proper subrings of the ring of integers that are also _____ s.

a. Order
b. Annihilator
c. Efficiency
d. Algebraic

15. In linear algebra, _____ is a version of Gaussian elimination that puts zeros both above and below each pivot element as it goes from the top row of the given matrix to the bottom. In other words, _____ brings a matrix to reduced row echelon form, whereas Gaussian elimination takes it only as far as row echelon form. Every matrix has a reduced row echelon form, and this algorithm is guaranteed to produce it.

a. Spheroidal wave functions
b. Conservation form
c. Gauss-Jordan elimination
d. Lax equivalence theorem

16. In linear algebra a matrix is in row echelon form if

- All nonzero rows are above any rows of all zeroes, and
- The leading coefficient of a row is always strictly to the right of the leading coefficient of the row above it.

This is the definition used in this article, but some texts add a third condition:

- The leading coefficient of each nonzero row is one.

A matrix is in _____ (also called row canonical form) if it satisfies the above three conditions, and if, in addition

- Every leading coefficient is the only nonzero entry in its column.

The first non-zero entry in each row is called a pivot.

This matrix is in _____:

$$\begin{bmatrix} 0 & 1 & 4 & 0 & 0 \\ 0 & 0 & 0 & 1 & 0 \\ 0 & 0 & 0 & 0 & 1 \\ 0 & 0 & 0 & 0 & 0 \end{bmatrix}.$$

The following matrix is also in row echelon form, but not in reduced row form:

$$\begin{bmatrix} 1 & 1 & 1 & 1 \\ 0 & 9 & 0 & 2 \\ 0 & 0 & 0 & 3 \end{bmatrix}.$$

However, this matrix is not in row echelon form, as the leading coefficient of row 3 is not strictly to the right of the leading coefficient of row 2.

$$\begin{bmatrix} 1 & 2 & 3 & 4 \\ 0 & 3 & 7 & 2 \\ 0 & 2 & 0 & 0 \end{bmatrix}$$

Every non-zero matrix can be reduced to an infinite number of echelon forms (they can all be multiples of each other, for example) via elementary matrix transformations.

a. Folded spectrum method
c. Reduced row echelon form

b. Pseudospectrum
d. Basic Linear Algebra Subprograms

17. In linear algebra a matrix is in _____ if

- All nonzero rows are above any rows of all zeroes, and
- The leading coefficient of a row is always strictly to the right of the leading coefficient of the row above it.

This is the definition used in this article, but some texts add a third condition:

- The leading coefficient of each nonzero row is one.

A matrix is in reduced _____ if it satisfies the above three conditions, and if, in addition

- Every leading coefficient is the only nonzero entry in its column.

The first non-zero entry in each row is called a pivot.

Chapter 4. Systems of Linear Equations; Matrices

This matrix is in reduced _____:

$$\begin{bmatrix} 0 & 1 & 4 & 0 & 0 \\ 0 & 0 & 0 & 1 & 0 \\ 0 & 0 & 0 & 0 & 1 \\ 0 & 0 & 0 & 0 & 0 \end{bmatrix}.$$

The following matrix is also in _____, but not in reduced row form:

$$\begin{bmatrix} 1 & 1 & 1 & 1 \\ 0 & 9 & 0 & 2 \\ 0 & 0 & 0 & 3 \end{bmatrix}.$$

However, this matrix is not in _____, as the leading coefficient of row 3 is not strictly to the right of the leading coefficient of row 2.

$$\begin{bmatrix} 1 & 2 & 3 & 4 \\ 0 & 3 & 7 & 2 \\ 0 & 2 & 0 & 0 \end{bmatrix}$$

Every non-zero matrix can be reduced to an infinite number of echelon forms via elementary matrix transformations.

a. Portable, Extensible Toolkit for Scientific Computation
b. Gaussian elimination
c. Reduced row echelon form
d. Row echelon form

18. In commutative algebra, the notions of an element _____ over a ring, and of an _____ extension of rings, are a generalization of the notions in field theory of an element being algebraic over a field, and of an algebraic extension of fields.

The special case of greatest interest in number theory is that of complex numbers _____ over the ring of integers Z.

The term ring will be understood to mean commutative ring with a unit.

a. Integral test for convergence
b. Integral
c. Arc length
d. Antidifferentiation

Chapter 4. Systems of Linear Equations; Matrices

19. A _____ is a deliberate process for transforming one or more inputs into one or more results, with variable change.

The term is used in a variety of senses, from the very definite arithmetical using an algorithm to the vague heuristics of calculating a strategy in a competition or calculating the chance of a successful relationship between two people.

Multiplying 7 by 8 is a simple algorithmic _____.

a. Calculation
c. Mathematical object
b. Mathematical maturity
d. Mathematics Subject Classification

20. _____ is the mathematical operation of scaling one number by another. It is one of the four basic operations in elementary arithmetic.

_____ is defined for whole numbers in terms of repeated addition; for example, 4 multiplied by 3 can be calculated by adding 3 copies of 4 together:

$$4 + 4 + 4 = 12.$$

_____ of rational numbers and real numbers is defined by systematic generalization of this basic idea.

a. The number 0 is even.
c. Multiplication
b. Least common multiple
d. Highest common factor

21. In economics, business, retail, and accounting, a _____ is the value of money that has been used up to produce something, and hence is not available for use anymore. In business, the _____ may be one of acquisition, in which case the amount of money expended to acquire it is counted as _____. In this case, money is the input that is gone in order to acquire the thing.

a. 2-3 heap
c. 120-cell
b. 1-center problem
d. Cost

22. In mathematics, the term _____ has several different important meanings:

- An _____ is an equality that remains true regardless of the values of any variables that appear within it, to distinguish it from an equality which is true under more particular conditions. For this, the 'triple bar' symbol ≡ is sometimes used.
- In algebra, an _____ or _____ element of a set S with a binary operation Â· is an element e that, when combined with any element x of S, produces that same x. That is, eÂ·x = xÂ·e = x for all x in S.
    - The _____ function from a set S to itself, often denoted id or id$_S$, s the function such that i = x for all x in S. This function serves as the _____ element in the set of all functions from S to itself with respect to function composition.
    - In linear algebra, the _____ matrix of size n is the n-by-n square matrix with ones on the main diagonal and zeros elsewhere. This matrix serves as the _____ with respect to matrix multiplication.

A common example of the first meaning is the trigonometric _____

$$\sin^2 \theta + \cos^2 \theta = 1$$

which is true for all real values of θ, as opposed to

$$\cos \theta = 1,$$

which is true only for some values of θ, not all. For example, the latter equation is true when $\theta = 0$, false when $\theta = 2$

The concepts of 'additive _____' and 'multiplicative _____' are central to the Peano axioms. The number 0 is the 'additive _____' for integers, real numbers, and complex numbers. For the real numbers, for all $a \in \mathbb{R}$,

$$0 + a = a,$$

$$a + 0 = a, \text{ and}$$

$$0 + 0 = 0.$$

Similarly, The number 1 is the 'multiplicative _____' for integers, real numbers, and complex numbers.

a. Identity
b. Action
c. Intersection
d. ARIA

23. In linear algebra, the _____ or unit matrix of size n is the n-by-n square matrix with ones on the main diagonal and zeros elsewhere. It is denoted by I_n, or simply by I if the size is immaterial or can be trivially determined by the context. (In some fields, such as quantum mechanics, the _____ is denoted by a boldface one, 1; otherwise it is identical to I.)
a. Associativity
b. Identity matrix
c. Unital
d. Arity

24. In mathematics, the _____ of a number n is the number that, when added to n, yields zero. The _____ of n is denoted −n. For example, 7 is −7, because 7 + (−7) = 0, and the _____ of −0.3 is 0.3, because −0.3 + 0.3 = 0.
a. Algebraic structure
b. Associativity
c. Arity
d. Additive inverse

25. In mathematics, a _____ for a number x, denoted by $\frac{1}{x}$ or x^{-1}, is a number which when multiplied by x yields the multiplicative identity, 1. The _____ of x is also called the reciprocal of x. The _____ of a fraction p/q is q/p.
a. Double exponential
b. Golden function
c. Hyperbolic function
d. Multiplicative inverse

Chapter 4. Systems of Linear Equations; Matrices

26. _____ is the practice and study of hiding information. In modern times, _____ is considered a branch of both mathematics and computer science, and is affiliated closely with information theory, computer security, and engineering. _____ is used in applications present in technologically advanced societies; examples include the security of ATM cards, computer passwords, and electronic commerce, which all depend on _____.
   a. MAGENTA
   b. LOKI
   c. Cryptography
   d. CIKS-1

27. In communication theory and coding theory, _____ is the process of translating received messages into codewords of a given code These methods are often used to recover messages sent over a noisy channel, such as a binary symmetric channel.
   a. Decoding
   b. Hilbert spectrum
   c. MUSHRA
   d. Fast Folding Algorithm

28. In mathematics the _____ of a set which is equipped with the operation of addition is an element which, when added to any element x in the set, yields x. One of the most familiar additive identities is the number 0 from elementary mathematics, but additive identities occur in other mathematical structures where addition is defined, such as in groups and rings.

   - The _____ familiar from elementary mathematics is zero, denoted 0. For example,

     $5 + 0 = 5 = 0 + 5$.

   - In the natural numbers N and all of its supersets, the _____ is 0. Thus for any one of these numbers n,

     $n + 0 = n = 0 + n$.

   Let N be a set which is closed under the operation of addition, denoted +. An _____ for N is any element e such that for any element n in N,

   $e + n = n = n + e$.

   a. Unit ring
   b. Additive identity
   c. Algebraically independent
   d. Unique factorization domain

29. In mathematics, _____ is a property that a binary operation can have. It means that, within an expression containing two or more of the same associative operators in a row, the order that the operations are performed does not matter as long as the sequence of the operands is not changed. That is, rearranging the parentheses in such an expression will not change its value.
   a. Unital
   b. Associativity
   c. Idempotence
   d. Algebraically closed

30. In mathematics, and in particular in abstract algebra, distributivity is a property of binary operations that generalises the _____ law from elementary algebra.
   a. Permutation
   b. Closure with a twist
   c. General linear group
   d. Distributive

31. In mathematics, a _____ is a constant multiplicative factor of a certain object. For example, in the expression $9x^2$, the _____ of x^2 is 9.

The object can be such things as a variable, a vector, a function, etc.

a. Stability radius
b. Multivariate division algorithm
c. Coefficient
d. Fibonacci polynomials

Chapter 5. Linear Inequalities and Linear Programming

1. In mathematics, _____ is a technique for optimization of a linear objective function, subject to linear equality and linear inequality constraints. Informally, _____ determines the way to achieve the best outcome in a given mathematical model given some list of requirements represented as linear equations.

More formally, given a polytope, and a real-valued affine function

$$f(x_1, x_2, \ldots, x_n) = c_1 x_1 + c_2 x_2 + \cdots + c_n x_n + d$$

defined on this polytope, a _____ method will find a point in the polytope where this function has the smallest value.

a. Descent direction
c. Lin-Kernighan
b. Linear programming
d. Linear programming relaxation

2. A _____ is a software program that facilitates symbolic mathematics. The core functionality of a CAS is manipulation of mathematical expressions in symbolic form.

Chapter 5. Linear Inequalities and Linear Programming

The symbolic manipulations supported typically include

- simplification to the smallest possible expression or some standard form, including automatic simplification with assumptions and simplification with constraints
- substitution of symbolic, functors or numeric values for expressions
- change of form of expressions: expanding products and powers, partial and full factorization, rewriting as partial fractions, constraint satisfaction, rewriting trigonometric functions as exponentials, etc.
- partial and total differentiation
- symbolic constrained and unconstrained global optimization
- solution of linear and some non-linear equations over various domains
- solution of some differential and difference equations
- taking some limits
- some indefinite and definite integration, including multidimensional integrals
- integral transforms
- arbitrary-precision numeric operations
- Series operations such as expansion, summation and products
- matrix operations including products, inverses, etc.
- display of mathematical expressions in two-dimensional mathematical form, often using typesetting systems similar to TeX
- add-ons for use in applied mathematics such as physics packages for physical computation
- plotting graphs and parametric plots of functions in two and three dimensions, and animating them
- APIs for linking it on an external program such as a database, or using in a programming language to use the _____
- drawing charts and diagrams
- string manipulation such as matching and searching
- statistical computation
- Theorem proving and verification
- graphic production and editing such as CGI and signal processing as image processing
- sound synthesis

Many also include a programming language, allowing users to implement their own algorithms.

Some _____ s focus on a specific area of application; these are typically developed in academia and are free.

a. 120-cell
c. 1-center problem
b. 2-3 heap
d. Computer algebra system

3. In mathematics, _____ and undefined are used to explain whether or not expressions have meaningful, sensible, and unambiguous values. Not all branches of mathematics come to the same conclusion.

The following expressions are undefined in all contexts, but remarks in the analysis section may apply.

a. Plugging in
b. Toy model
c. Defined
d. LHS

4. _____ is either of the two parts into which a plane divides the three-dimensional space. More generally, a _____ is either of the two parts into which a hyperplane divides an affine space.
   a. Parallelogram law
   b. Half-space
   c. Simple polytope
   d. Pendent

5. In mathematics, the _____ H is the set of complex numbers

$$\mathbb{H} = \{x + iy \,|\, y < 0; x, y \in \mathbb{R}\}$$

with positive imaginary part y. Other names are hyperbolic plane, Poincaré plane and Lobachevsky plane, particularly in texts by Russian authors. Some authors prefer the symbol $\mathfrak{h}$.

- Upper half-plane
- Cusp neighborhood
- Fuchsian group
- Fundamental domain
- Hyperbolic geometry
- Kleinian group
- Modular group
- Poincaré metric
- Riemann surface
- Schwarz-Ahlfors-Pick theorem

a. Cauchy-Hadamard theorem
b. Lower half-plane
c. Bieberbach conjecture
d. Principal branch

6. In mathematics, the _____ H is the set of complex numbers

$$\mathbb{H} = \{x + iy \,|\, y > 0; x, y \in \mathbb{R}\}$$

with positive imaginary part y.

The term is associated with a common visualization of complex numbers with points in the plane endowed with Cartesian coordinates, with the Y-axis pointing upwards: the '_____' corresponds to the half-plane above the X-axis.

When endowed with a particular metric, the _____ may be called the hyperbolic plane, Poincaré half-plane, or Lobachevsky plane, particularly in texts by Russian authors.

Chapter 5. Linear Inequalities and Linear Programming

a. Analytic continuation
b. Analytic capacity
c. Argument principle
d. Upper half-plane

7. In mathematics, an _____ is a statement about the relative size or order of two objects, or about whether they are the same or not

- The notation a < b means that a is less than b.
- The notation a > b means that a is greater than b.
- The notation a ≠ b means that a is not equal to b, but does not say that one is bigger than the other or even that they can be compared in size.

In all these cases, a is not equal to b, hence, '_____'.

These relations are known as strict _____

- The notation a ≤ b means that a is less than or equal to b;
- The notation a ≥ b means that a is greater than or equal to b;

An additional use of the notation is to show that one quantity is much greater than another, normally by several orders of magnitude.

- The notation a << b means that a is much less than b.
- The notation a >> b means that a is much greater than b.

If the sense of the _____ is the same for all values of the variables for which its members are defined, then the _____ is called an 'absolute' or 'unconditional' _____. If the sense of an _____ holds only for certain values of the variables involved, but is reversed or destroyed for other values of the variables, it is called a conditional _____.

An _____ may appear unsolvable because it only states whether a number is larger or smaller than another number; but it is possible to apply the same operations for equalities to inequalities. For example, to find x for the _____ 10x > 23 one would divide 23 by 10.

a. Inequality
b. A Mathematical Theory of Communication
c. A posteriori
d. A chemical equation

8. A _____ is an algebraic equation in which each term is either a constant or the product of a constant and a single variable. _____s can have one, two, three or more variables.

_____s occur with great regularity in applied mathematics.

a. Quadratic equation
b. Linear equation
c. Quartic equation
d. Difference of two squares

Chapter 5. Linear Inequalities and Linear Programming

9. A set S of real numbers is called _____ from above if there is a real number k such that k ≥ s for all s in S. The number k is called an upper bound of S. The terms _____ from below and lower bound are similarly defined.
    a. Descent
    b. Derivative algebra
    c. Harmonic series
    d. Bounded

10. In optimization, a candidate solution is a member of a set of possible solutions to a given problem. A candidate solution does not have to be a likely or reasonable solution to the problem. The space of all candidate solutions is called the _____, feasible set, search space, or solution space.
    a. Leapfrog integration
    b. Step response
    c. Quadratic eigenvalue problem
    d. Feasible region

11. _____ is an important tool for manufacturing and engineering, where it can have a major impact on the productivity of a process. In manufacturing, the purpose of _____ is to minimize the production time and costs, by telling a production facility what to make, when, with which staff, and on which equipment. Production _____ aims to maximize the efficiency of the operation and reduce costs.
    a. Critical point
    b. Boolean algebra
    c. Crib
    d. Scheduling

12. An _____ is a tree data structure in which each internal node has up to eight children. _____s are most often used to partition a three dimensional space by recursively subdividing it into eight octants. _____s are the three-dimensional analog of quadtrees.
    a. External node
    b. Octree
    c. Interval tree
    d. Adaptive k-d tree

13. In mathematics, a _____ is a condition that a solution to an optimization problem must satisfy. There are two types of _____s: equality _____s and inequality _____s. The set of solutions that satisfy all _____s is called the feasible set.
    a. Decidable
    b. Foci
    c. Concurrent
    d. Constraint

14. The mathematical concept of a _____ expresses the intuitive idea of deterministic dependence between two quantities, one of which is viewed as primary and the other as secondary. A _____ then is a way to associate a unique output for each input of a specified type, for example, a real number or an element of a given set.
    a. Going up
    b. Function
    c. Grill
    d. Coherent

15. A _____ is an abstract model that uses mathematical language to describe the behavior of a system. Eykhoff defined a _____ as 'a representation of the essential aspects of an existing system which presents knowledge of that system in usable form'.
    a. Total least squares
    b. Mathematical model
    c. Metaheuristic
    d. Rata Die

16. _____ is an economics theory, that refers to individuals or societies gaining the maximum amount out of the resources they have available to them. The theory proposed by most economists is that _____ refers to the _____ of profit.

As some economists have begun to find out, this theory does not hold true for all people and cultures.

a. Composite
b. Boundary
c. Homogeneity
d. Maximization

17. In mathematics and computer science, an optimization problem is the problem of finding the best solution from all feasible solutions. More formally, an optimization problem A is a quadruple , where

- I is a set of instances;
- given an instance >, f is the set of feasible solutions;
- given an instance x and a feasible solution y of x, m denotes the measure of y, which is usually a positive real.
- g is the goal function, and is either min or max.

The goal is then to find for some instance x an _________, that is, a feasible solution y with

>

For each optimization problem, there is a corresponding decision problem that asks whether there is a feasible solution for some particular measure m_0. For example, if there is a graph G which contains vertices u and v, an optimization problem might be 'find a path from u to v that uses the fewest edges'. This problem might have an answer of, say, 4.

a. Exponential time
b. Interactive proof system
c. Approximation algorithms
d. Optimal solution

18. In mathematics, a _________ is a statement that can be proved on the basis of explicitly stated or previously agreed assumptions.

a. Disjunction introduction
b. Logical value
c. Boolean function
d. Theorem

Chapter 6. Linear Programming: Simplex Method

1. In mathematics, _____ is a technique for optimization of a linear objective function, subject to linear equality and linear inequality constraints. Informally, _____ determines the way to achieve the best outcome in a given mathematical model given some list of requirements represented as linear equations.

More formally, given a polytope, and a real-valued affine function

$$f(x_1, x_2, \ldots, x_n) = c_1 x_1 + c_2 x_2 + \cdots + c_n x_n + d$$

defined on this polytope, a _____ method will find a point in the polytope where this function has the smallest value.

   a. Linear programming
   c. Lin-Kernighan
   b. Descent direction
   d. Linear programming relaxation

2. In geometry, a _____ or n-_____ is an n-dimensional analogue of a triangle. Specifically, a _____ is the convex hull of a set of affinely independent points in some Euclidean space of dimension n or higher.

For example, a 0-_____ is a point, a 1-_____ is a line segment, a 2-_____ is a triangle, a 3-_____ is a tetrahedron, and a 4-_____ is a pentachoron.

   a. Demihypercubes
   c. Polytetrahedron
   b. Hypercell
   d. Simplex

3. In mathematical optimization theory, the simplex algorithm, created by the American mathematician George Dantzig in 1947, is a popular algorithm for numerical solution of the linear programming problem. The journal Computing in Science and Engineering listed it as one of the top 10 algorithms of the century.

An unrelated, but similarly named method is the Nelder-Mead method or downhill _____ due to Nelder ' Mead and is a numerical method for optimising many-dimensional unconstrained problems, belonging to the more general class of search algorithms.

   a. Hill climbing
   c. Simplex method
   b. Differential evolution
   d. Fibonacci search

4. A _____ is a software program that facilitates symbolic mathematics. The core functionality of a CAS is manipulation of mathematical expressions in symbolic form.

Chapter 6. Linear Programming: Simplex Method

The symbolic manipulations supported typically include

- simplification to the smallest possible expression or some standard form, including automatic simplification with assumptions and simplification with constraints
- substitution of symbolic, functors or numeric values for expressions
- change of form of expressions: expanding products and powers, partial and full factorization, rewriting as partial fractions, constraint satisfaction, rewriting trigonometric functions as exponentials, etc.
- partial and total differentiation
- symbolic constrained and unconstrained global optimization
- solution of linear and some non-linear equations over various domains
- solution of some differential and difference equations
- taking some limits
- some indefinite and definite integration, including multidimensional integrals
- integral transforms
- arbitrary-precision numeric operations
- Series operations such as expansion, summation and products
- matrix operations including products, inverses, etc.
- display of mathematical expressions in two-dimensional mathematical form, often using typesetting systems similar to TeX
- add-ons for use in applied mathematics such as physics packages for physical computation
- plotting graphs and parametric plots of functions in two and three dimensions, and animating them
- APIs for linking it on an external program such as a database, or using in a programming language to use the _____
- drawing charts and diagrams
- string manipulation such as matching and searching
- statistical computation
- Theorem proving and verification
- graphic production and editing such as CGI and signal processing as image processing
- sound synthesis

Many also include a programming language, allowing users to implement their own algorithms.

Some _____s focus on a specific area of application; these are typically developed in academia and are free.

a. 120-cell
c. 2-3 heap
b. Computer algebra system
d. 1-center problem

5. In mathematics, _____ and undefined are used to explain whether or not expressions have meaningful, sensible, and unambiguous values. Not all branches of mathematics come to the same conclusion.

The following expressions are undefined in all contexts, but remarks in the analysis section may apply.

a. LHS	b. Plugging in
c. Toy model	d. Defined

6. _____ is an economics theory, that refers to individuals or societies gaining the maximum amount out of the resources they have available to them. The theory proposed by most economists is that _____ refers to the _____ of profit.

As some economists have begun to find out, this theory does not hold true for all people and cultures.

a. Homogeneity	b. Boundary
c. Composite	d. Maximization

7. _____, also sometimes known as standard form or as exponential notation, is a way of writing numbers that accommodates values too large or small to be conveniently written in standard decimal notation. _____ has a number of useful properties and is often favored by scientists, mathematicians and engineers, who work with such numbers.

In _____, numbers are written in the form:

$$a \times 10^b$$

a. Scientific notation	b. Radix point
c. 1-center problem	d. Leading zero

8. In Linear programming a _____ is a variable which is added to a constraint to turn the inequality into an equation. This is required to turn an inequality into an equality where a linear combination of variables is less than or equal to a given constant in the former. As with the other variables in the augmented constraints, the _____ cannot take on negative values, as the Simplex algorithm requires them to be positive or zero.

a. Shekel function	b. Shape optimization
c. Slack variable	d. Bellman equation

9. In optimization, a candidate solution is a member of a set of possible solutions to a given problem. A candidate solution does not have to be a likely or reasonable solution to the problem. The space of all candidate solutions is called the _____, feasible set, search space, or solution space.

a. Quadratic eigenvalue problem	b. Step response
c. Feasible region	d. Leapfrog integration

10. In mathematics, a _____ is a statement that can be proved on the basis of explicitly stated or previously agreed assumptions.

a. Disjunction introduction	b. Logical value
c. Boolean function	d. Theorem

11. Initial objects are also called _____, and terminal objects are also called final.

a. Direct limit	b. Terminal object
c. Coterminal	d. Colimit

Chapter 6. Linear Programming: Simplex Method

12. In mathematics, a _____ is a condition that a solution to an optimization problem must satisfy. There are two types of _____s: equality _____s and inequality _____s. The set of solutions that satisfy all _____s is called the feasible set.
    a. Decidable
    b. Concurrent
    c. Foci
    d. Constraint

13. In mathematical optimization theory, the _____, created by the North American mathematician George Dantzig in 1947, is a popular technique for numerical solution of the linear programming problem.
    a. Simplex algorithm
    b. Feit–Thompson theorem
    c. Partition
    d. Sociable number

14. In mathematics, an _____ or member of a set is any one of the distinct objects that make up that set.

Writing A = {1,2,3,4}, means that the _____s of the set A are the numbers 1, 2, 3 and 4. Groups of _____s of A, for example {1,2}, are subsets of A.

    a. Order
    b. Universal code
    c. Ideal
    d. Element

15. In mathematics, especially functional analysis, a hermitian element A of a C*-algebra is a _____ if its spectrum consists of nonnegative real numbers. It is possible to prove that an element x of a C*-algebra A is positive if and only if there is some b in A such that x = b*b.

If A is a bounded linear operator on a Hilbert space H, then this notion coincides with the condition that A is self-adjoint and $\langle Ax, x \rangle$ is nonnegative for every vector x in H.

    a. Positive element
    b. C_0-semigroup
    c. Gelfand representation
    d. Monotonic

16. In the mathematical area of order theory, every partially ordered set P gives rise to a _____ partially ordered set which is often denoted by P^{op} or P^d. This _____ order P^{op} is defined to be the set with the inverse order. It is easy to see that this construction, which can be depicted by flipping the Hasse diagram for P upside down, will indeed yield a partially ordered set.
    a. Contraction mapping
    b. Christofides heuristics
    c. Context-sensitive language
    d. Dual

17. In linear programming, the primary problem and the _____ are complementary. A solution to either one determines a solution to both.

Linear programming problems are optimization problems in which the objective function and the constraints are all linear.

    a. Dual problem
    b. Linear matrix inequality
    c. Linear programming relaxation
    d. Topological derivative

18. In linear algebra, the _____ of a matrix A is another matrix A^T created by any one of the following equivalent actions:

- write the rows of A as the columns of A^T
- write the columns of A as the rows of A^T
- reflect A by its main diagonal to obtain A^T

Formally, the _____ of an m × n matrix A is the n × m matrix

$$A^T_{ij} = A_{ji} \text{ for } 1 \leq i \leq n, 1 \leq j \leq m.$$

- $\begin{bmatrix} 1 & 2 \\ 3 & 4 \end{bmatrix}^T = \begin{bmatrix} 1 & 3 \\ 2 & 4 \end{bmatrix}.$

- $\begin{bmatrix} 1 & 2 \\ 3 & 4 \\ 5 & 6 \end{bmatrix}^T = \begin{bmatrix} 1 & 3 & 5 \\ 2 & 4 & 6 \end{bmatrix}.$

For matrices A, B and scalar c we have the following properties of _____:

1. $\left(A^T\right)^T = A$

   Taking the _____ is an involution.

- $(A + B)^T = A^T + B^T$

   The _____ respects addition.

- $(AB)^T = B^T A^T$

   Note that the order of the factors reverses. From this one can deduce that a square matrix A is invertible if and only if A^T is invertible, and in this case we have^T =$^{-1}$. It is relatively easy to extend this result to the general case of multiple matrices, where we find that^T = $Z^T Y^T X^T ... C^T B^T A^T$.

- $(cA)^T = cA^T$

Chapter 6. Linear Programming: Simplex Method

The _____ of a scalar is the same scalar. Together with, this states that the _____ is a linear map from the space of m × n matrices to the space of all n × m matrices.

- $\det(\mathbf{A}^T) = \det(\mathbf{A})$

  The determinant of a matrix is the same as that of its _____.

- The dot product of two column vectors a and b can be computed as

$$\mathbf{a} \cdot \mathbf{b} = \mathbf{a}^T \mathbf{b},$$

which is written as $a_i \, b^i$ in Einstein notation.
- If A has only real entries, then $A^T A$ is a positive-semidefinite matrix.
- $(\mathbf{A}^T)^{-1} = (\mathbf{A}^{-1})^T$

  The _____ of an invertible matrix is also invertible, and its inverse is the _____ of the inverse of the original matrix.

- If A is a square matrix, then its eigenvalues are equal to the eigenvalues of its _____.

A square matrix whose _____ is equal to itself is called a symmetric matrix; that is, A is symmetric if

$$\mathbf{A}^T = \mathbf{A}.$$

A square matrix whose _____ is also its inverse is called an orthogonal matrix; that is, G is orthogonal if

$$\mathbf{G}\mathbf{G}^T = \mathbf{G}^T\mathbf{G} = \mathbf{I}_n, \text{ the identity matrix.}$$

A square matrix whose _____ is equal to its negative is called skew-symmetric matrix; that is, A is skew-symmetric if

$$\mathbf{A}^T = -\mathbf{A}.$$

The conjugate _____ of the complex matrix A, written as A^*, is obtained by taking the _____ of A and the complex conjugate of each entry:

$$\mathbf{A}^* = (\overline{\mathbf{A}})^T = \overline{(\mathbf{A}^T)}.$$

If f: V→W is a linear map between vector spaces V and W with nondegenerate bilinear forms, we define the _____ of f to be the linear map $^t f$: W→V, determined by

$$B_V(v, {}^t f(w)) = B_W(f(v), w) \quad \forall \ v \in V, w \in W.$$

Here, B_V and B_W are the bilinear forms on V and W respectively. The matrix of the _____ of a map is the transposed matrix only if the bases are orthonormal with respect to their bilinear forms.

Over a complex vector space, one often works with sesquilinear forms instead of bilinear.

a. Transpose
c. Cartan matrix
b. Tridiagonal matrix
d. Polynomial matrix

19. In mathematics, a _____ is a rectangular table of elements, which may be numbers or, more generally, any abstract quantities that can be added and multiplied. Matrices are used to describe linear equations, keep track of the coefficients of linear transformations and to record data that depend on multiple parameters. Matrices are described by the field of _____ theory.

a. Matrix
c. Compression
b. Coherent
d. Double counting

20. In the geometry of the projective plane, _____ refers to geometric transformations that replace points by lines and lines by points while preserving incidence properties among the transformed objects. The existence of such transformations leads to a general principle, that any theorem about incidences between points and lines in the projective plane may be transformed into another theorem about lines and points, by a substitution of the appropriate words.

_____ in the projective plane is a special case of _____ for projective spaces, transformations that interchange

dimension + codimension.

a. Disk
c. Blocking
b. Decidable
d. Duality

21. In Linear programming a _____ is a variable which is subtracted from a constraint to turn the inequality into an equation.

This is required to turn an inequality into an equality where a linear combination of variables is greater than or equal to a given constant in the former. As with the other variables in the augmented constraints, the _____ cannot take on negative values, as the Simplex algorithm requires them to be positive or zero.

a. Surplus variable
c. Global optimum
b. Quantum annealing
d. Successive linear programming

Chapter 7. Logic, Sets, and Counting

1. _____ is the study of the principles of valid demonstration and inference. _____ is a branch of philosophy, a part of the classical trivium of grammar, _____, and rhetoric. of λογικÏŒς, 'possessed of reason, intellectual, dialectical, argumentative', from λÏŒγος logos, 'word, thought, idea, argument, account, reason, or principle'.
   a. Counterpart theory
   b. Satisfiability
   c. Boolean function
   d. Logic

2. In logic and mathematics, _____ or not is an operation on logical values, for example, the logical value of a proposition, that sends true to false and false to true. Intuitively, the _____ of a proposition holds exactly when that proposition does not hold. In grammar, nor is an adverb which acts as a coordinating conjunction.
   a. Syntax
   b. 1-center problem
   c. Sentence diagram
   d. Negation

3. In logic and philosophy, _____ refers to either (a) the 'content' or 'meaning' of a meaningful declarative sentence or (b) the pattern of symbols, marks, or sounds that make up a meaningful declarative sentence. _____s in either case are intended to be truth-bearers, that is, they are either true or false.

   The existence of _____s in the former sense, as well as the existence of 'meanings', is disputed.

   a. Proposition
   b. Linear logic
   c. Laws of classical logic
   d. Logicism

4. In logic and mathematics, or, also known as logical _____ or inclusive _____ is a logical operator that results in true whenever one or more of its operands are true. In grammar, or is a coordinating conjunction. In ordinary language 'or' rather has the meaning of exclusive _____.
   a. Triquetra
   b. Disjunction
   c. Cube
   d. Zero-point energy

5. In propositional logic, contraposition is a logical relationship between two statements of material implication. A proposition Q is materially implied by a proposition P when the following relationship holds:

$$(P \rightarrow Q)$$

In vernacular terms, this states 'If P then Q', or, 'If Socrates is a man then Socrates is human.' In a conditional such as this, P is called the antecedent and Q the consequent. One statement is the _____ of the other just when its antecedent is the negated consequent of the other, and vice-versa.

   a. Contour map
   b. Control chart
   c. Continuous signal
   d. Contrapositive

6. _____ is a concept in traditional logic referring to a 'type of immediate inference in which from a given proposition another proposition is inferred which has as its subject the predicate of the original proposition and as its predicate the subject of the original proposition (the quality of the proposition being retained).'
   a. Field
   b. Boolean algebra
   c. Foci
   d. Converse Logic

Chapter 7. Logic, Sets, and Counting

7. A _____ is a mathematical table used in logic -- specifically in connection with Boolean algebra, boolean functions, and propositional calculus -- to compute the functional values of logical expressions on each of their functional arguments, that is, on each combination of values taken by their logical variables. In particular, _____s can be used to tell whether a propositional expression is true for all legitimate input values, that is, logically valid.

The pattern of reasoning that the _____ tabulates was Frege's, Peirce's, and Schröder's by 1880.

- a. 1-center problem
- b. 2-3 heap
- c. 120-cell
- d. Truth table

8. In mathematics, _____ and undefined are used to explain whether or not expressions have meaningful, sensible, and unambiguous values. Not all branches of mathematics come to the same conclusion.

The following expressions are undefined in all contexts, but remarks in the analysis section may apply.

- a. LHS
- b. Toy model
- c. Plugging in
- d. Defined

9. In logic and mathematics, _____ is a logical relation that holds between a set T of formulae and a formula B when every model of T is also a model of B. In symbols,

1. $T \models B$
2. $T \Rightarrow B$
3. $T \therefore B$

which may be read 'T implies B, or 'B is a consequence of T'. In such an implication, T is called the antecedent, while B is called the consequent.

In other words, holds when the class of models of T is a subset of the class of models of B.

- a. Proposition
- b. Necessary and sufficient
- c. Thoralf Albert Skolem
- d. Logical implication

10. In philosophy and logic, _____ is the status of facts that are not logically necessarily true or false.

Chapter 7. Logic, Sets, and Counting

In philosophy and logic, people draw a distinction between

- possibility: 'If it happened, it must be possible' -- If an event happened, it must be a possible event. A possible statement is not necessarily false. A 'possibility', such as a coincidence, is either a '_____', or a 'necessity' (but not both.)
- _____: a contingent event is an event which 'could have not happened'. Each contingent event is also a possible event, but not vice versa. A contingent statement is not necessarily false, but it is not necessarily true either.
- necessity: a necessary event is an event which 'could not have not happened'. In other words, a necessary event inevitably must have happened. Each necessary event is also a possible event, but not vice versa. A necessary statement is a statement that is necessarily true, such as a tautology.

a. Rigid designator
b. Modal companion
c. Modal operator
d. Contingency

11. _____ In logic, statements p and q are logically equivalent if they have the same logical content.
   a. Fallacies of definition
   b. Realizability
   c. Logical equivalence
   d. Distribution rule

12. In mathematics, an _____ or member of a set is any one of the distinct objects that make up that set.

Writing A = {1,2,3,4}, means that the _____s of the set A are the numbers 1, 2, 3 and 4. Groups of _____s of A, for example {1,2}, are subsets of A.

a. Ideal
b. Order
c. Element
d. Universal code

13. In mathematics, and more specifically set theory, the _____ is the unique set having no members. Some axiomatic set theories assure that the _____ exists by including an axiom of _____; in other theories, its existence can be deduced. Many possible properties of sets are trivially true for the _____.
   a. A Mathematical Theory of Communication
   b. Inverse function
   c. Empty function
   d. Empty set

14. In mathematics, a _____ is a set that is negligible in some sense. For different applications, the meaning of 'negligible' varies. In measure theory, any set of measure 0 is called a _____.
   a. Prevalence and shyness
   b. Borel-Cantelli lemma
   c. Null set
   d. Radonifying function

15. _____ is a branch of mathematics which focuses on the study of matrices. Initially a sub-branch of linear algebra, it has grown to cover subjects related to graph theory, algebra, combinatorics, and statistics as well.

The term matrix was first coined in 1848 by J.J. Sylvester as a name of an array of numbers.

a. Pairing
b. Semi-simple operators
c. Segre classification
d. Matrix theory

16. In mathematics, especially in set theory, a set A is a _____ of a set B if A is 'contained' inside B. Notice that A and B may coincide. The relationship of one set being a _____ of another is called inclusion.
   a. Horizontal line test
   b. Set of all sets
   c. Cartesian product
   d. Subset

17. In mathematics, two sets are said to be disjoint if they have no element in common. For example, {1, 2, 3} and {4, 5, 6} are _____.

Formally, two sets A and B are disjoint if their intersection is the empty set.
wikimedia.org/math/b/3/5/b35d3befc06b831ff4d6cd63bf922efb.png">

This definition extends to any collection of sets.

   a. Disjoint sets
   b. Horizontal line test
   c. Preimage
   d. Subset

18. In mathematics, the _____ of two sets A and B is the set that contains all elements of A that also belong to B, but no other elements.

For explanation of the symbols used in this article, refer to the table of mathematical symbols.

The _____ of A and B

The _____ of A and B is written 'A ∩ B'. Formally:

   x is an element of A ∩ B if and only if
   - x is an element of A and
   - x is an element of B.

   For example:
   - The _____ of the sets {1, 2, 3} and {2, 3, 4} is {2, 3}.
   - The number 9 is not in the _____ of the set of prime numbers {2, 3, 5, 7, 11, …} and the set of odd numbers {1, 3, 5, 7, 9, 11, …}.

If the _____ of two sets A and B is empty, that is they have no elements in common, then they are said to be disjoint, denoted: A ∩ B = Ø. For example the sets {1, 2} and {3, 4} are disjoint, written {1, 2} ∩ {3, 4} = Ø.

   a. Order
   b. Intersection
   c. Advice
   d. Erlang

Chapter 7. Logic, Sets, and Counting

19. In set theory, the term _____ refers to a set operation used in the convergence of set elements to form a resultant set containing the elements of both sets. As a simple example, a _____ of two disjoint sets, which do not have elements in common results in a set containing all elements from both sets. A Venn diagram representing the _____ of sets A and B.
    a. Introduction
    b. UES
    c. Event
    d. Union

20. _____ or set diagrams are diagrams that show all hypothetically possible logical relations between a finite collection of sets. _____ were invented around 1880 by John Venn. They are used in many fields, including set theory, probability, logic, statistics, and computer science.
    a. 2-3 heap
    b. 120-cell
    c. 1-center problem
    d. Venn diagrams

21. A _____ is a 2D geometric symbolic representation of information according to some visualization technique. Sometimes, the technique uses a 3D visualization which is then projected onto the 2D surface. The word graph is sometimes used as a synonym for _____.
    a. 2-3 heap
    b. 120-cell
    c. Diagram
    d. 1-center problem

22. _____ is the mathematical operation of scaling one number by another. It is one of the four basic operations in elementary arithmetic.

    _____ is defined for whole numbers in terms of repeated addition; for example, 4 multiplied by 3 can be calculated by adding 3 copies of 4 together:

    $$4 + 4 + 4 = 12.$$

    _____ of rational numbers and real numbers is defined by systematic generalization of this basic idea.

    a. Highest common factor
    b. Multiplication
    c. The number 0 is even.
    d. Least common multiple

23. In mathematics, a _____ is a statement that can be proved on the basis of explicitly stated or previously agreed assumptions.
    a. Disjunction introduction
    b. Theorem
    c. Logical value
    d. Boolean function

24. In information theory, a _____ is a function mapping an alphabet to non-negative real numbers, satisfying a generalization of Kraft's inequality. A _____ page, a type of character encoding table, is one such _____.
    a. Link encryption
    b. File Camouflage
    c. Deterministic encryption
    d. Code

25. In telecommunication, a _____ is an element of a code. Each _____ is a sequence of symbols assembled in accordance with the specific rules of the code and assigned a unique meaning.

Main article: Coding Theory

Coding Theory is the branch of mathematics that covers source codes and channel codes.

a. Code word
b. Gray code
c. Viterbi decoder
d. Parity bit

26. In mathematics, the _____ of a non-negative integer n, denoted by n!, is the product of all positive integers less than or equal to n. For example,

$$5! = 1 \times 2 \times 3 \times 4 \times 5 = 120$$

and
$$6! = 1 \times 2 \times 3 \times 4 \times 5 \times 6 = 720$$

The notation n! was introduced by Christian Kramp in 1808.

The _____ function is formally defined by

$$n! = \prod_{k=1}^{n} k \qquad \forall n \in \mathbb{N}.$$

The above definition incorporates the instance

$$0! = 1$$

as an instance of the fact that the product of no numbers at all is 1.

a. Factorial
b. Plane partition
c. Symbolic combinatorics
d. Partition of a set

27. _____ is usually defined as the activity of using and developing computer technology, computer hardware and software. It is the computer-specific part of information technology. Computer science (or _____ science) is the study and the science of the theoretical foundations of information and computation and their implementation and application in computer systems.

a. Probabilistic Turing Machine
b. Computing
c. Deterministic finite state machine
d. Parallel Random Access Machine

28. In several fields of mathematics the term _____ is used with different but closely related meanings. They all relate to the notion of mapping the elements of a set to other elements of the same set, i.e., exchanging elements of a set.

The general concept of _____ can be defined more formally in different contexts:

Chapter 7. Logic, Sets, and Counting

In combinatorics, a _____ is usually understood to be a sequence containing each element from a finite set once, and only once.

a. Linearly independent
c. Cyclic permutation
b. Tensor product
d. Permutation

29. In category theory, an abstract branch of mathematics, an _____ of a category C is an object I in C such that for every object X in C, there exists precisely one morphism I → X. The dual notion is that of a terminal object: T is terminal if for every object X in C there exists a single morphism X → T. _____s are also called coterminal, and terminal objects are also called final.

a. A chemical equation
c. A posteriori
b. A Mathematical Theory of Communication
d. Initial object

30. In computational complexity theory, an algorithm is said to take _____ if the asymptotic upper bound for the time it requires is proportional to the size of the input, which is usually denoted n.

Informally spoken, the running time increases linearly with the size of the input. For example, a procedure that adds up all elements of a list requires time proportional to the length of the list.

a. Truth table reduction
c. Time-constructible function
b. Constructible function
d. Linear time

31. In combinatorial mathematics, a _____ is an un-ordered collection of distinct elements, usually of a prescribed size and taken from a given set. Given such a set S, a _____ of elements of S is just a subset of S, where as always forsets the order of the elements is not taken into account. Also, as always forsets, no elements can be repeated more than once in a _____; this is often referred to as a 'collection without repetition'.

a. Combination
c. Heawood number
b. Fill-in
d. Sparsity

32. A _____ is a software program that facilitates symbolic mathematics. The core functionality of a CAS is manipulation of mathematical expressions in symbolic form.

The symbolic manipulations supported typically include

- simplification to the smallest possible expression or some standard form, including automatic simplification with assumptions and simplification with constraints
- substitution of symbolic, functors or numeric values for expressions
- change of form of expressions: expanding products and powers, partial and full factorization, rewriting as partial fractions, constraint satisfaction, rewriting trigonometric functions as exponentials, etc.
- partial and total differentiation
- symbolic constrained and unconstrained global optimization
- solution of linear and some non-linear equations over various domains
- solution of some differential and difference equations
- taking some limits
- some indefinite and definite integration, including multidimensional integrals
- integral transforms
- arbitrary-precision numeric operations
- Series operations such as expansion, summation and products
- matrix operations including products, inverses, etc.
- display of mathematical expressions in two-dimensional mathematical form, often using typesetting systems similar to TeX
- add-ons for use in applied mathematics such as physics packages for physical computation
- plotting graphs and parametric plots of functions in two and three dimensions, and animating them
- APIs for linking it on an external program such as a database, or using in a programming language to use the _____
- drawing charts and diagrams
- string manipulation such as matching and searching
- statistical computation
- Theorem proving and verification
- graphic production and editing such as CGI and signal processing as image processing
- sound synthesis

Many also include a programming language, allowing users to implement their own algorithms.

Some _____ s focus on a specific area of application; these are typically developed in academia and are free.

a. 120-cell
c. 1-center problem
b. 2-3 heap
d. Computer algebra system

Chapter 8. Probability

1. _____ IPA: [pjɛʁ dɛ™fɛʁ 'ma] (17 August 1601 or 1607/8 - 12 January 1665) was a French lawyer at the Parlement of Toulouse, France, and a mathematician who is given credit for early developments that led to modern calculus. In particular, he is recognized for his discovery of an original method of finding the greatest and the smallest ordinates of curved lines, which is analogous to that of the then unknown differential calculus, as well as his research into the theory of numbers. He also made notable contributions to analytic geometry, probability, and optics.
   - a. Felix Hausdorff
   - b. Nikita Borisov
   - c. Philip J. Davis
   - d. Pierre de Fermat

2. The word _____ denotes information gained by means of observation, experience as opposed to theoretical. A central concept in science and the scientific method is that all evidence must be _____ that is, dependent on evidence or consequences that are observable by the senses. It is usually differentiated from the philosophic usage of empiricism by the use of the adjective '_____' or the adverb 'empirically.' '_____' as an adjective or adverb is used in conjunction with both the natural and social sciences, and refers to the use of working hypotheses that are testable using observation or experiment.
   - a. A posteriori
   - b. A chemical equation
   - c. Empirical
   - d. A Mathematical Theory of Communication

3. _____ is the likelihood or chance that something is the case or will happen. Theoretical _____ is used extensively in areas such as statistics, mathematics, science and philosophy to draw conclusions about the likelihood of potential events and the underlying mechanics of complex systems.

   The word _____ does not have a consistent direct definition.
   - a. Statistical significance
   - b. Discrete random variable
   - c. Standardized moment
   - d. Probability

4. _____ is the branch of mathematics concerned with analysis of random phenomena. The central objects of _____ are random variables, stochastic processes, and events: mathematical abstractions of non-deterministic events or measured quantities that may either be single occurrences or evolve over time in an apparently random fashion. Although an individual coin toss or the roll of a die is a random event, if repeated many times the sequence of random events will exhibit certain statistical patterns, which can be studied and predicted.
   - a. Martingale central limit theorem
   - b. Standard probability space
   - c. Law of large numbers
   - d. Probability theory

5. The word _____ has many distinct meanings in different fields of knowledge, depending on their methodologies and the context of discussion. Broadly speaking we can say that a _____ is some kind of belief or claim that (supposedly) explains, asserts, or consolidates some class of claims. Additionally, in contrast with a theorem the statement of the _____ is generally accepted only in some tentative fashion as opposed to regarding it as having been conclusively established.
   - a. Theory
   - b. Defined
   - c. Transport of structure
   - d. Per mil

6. In probability theory, an _____ is a set of outcomes to which a probability is assigned. Typically, when the sample space is finite, any subset of the sample space is an _____. However, this approach does not work well in cases where the sample space is infinite, most notably when the outcome is a real number.

a. Equaliser b. Audio compression
c. Information set d. Event

7. In scientific inquiry, an _____ is a method of investigating particular types of research questions or solving particular types of problems. The _____ is a cornerstone in the empirical approach to acquiring deeper knowledge about the world and is used in both natural sciences as well as in social sciences. An _____ is defined, in science, as a method of investigating less known fields, solving practical problems and proving theoretical assumptions.

a. A Mathematical Theory of Communication b. A posteriori
c. Experiment d. A chemical equation

8. In statistics, a _____ is a subset of a population. Typically, the population is very large, making a census or a complete enumeration of all the values in the population impractical or impossible. The _____ represents a subset of manageable size.

a. Dispersion b. Duality
c. Boussinesq approximation d. Sample

9. In probability theory, the _____ or universal _____, often denoted S, Ω of an experiment or random trial is the set of all possible outcomes. For example, if the experiment is tossing a coin, the _____ is the set {head, tail}. For tossing a single six-sided die, the _____ is {1, 2, 3, 4, 5, 6}.

a. Martingale central limit theorem b. Marginal distribution
c. Markov chain d. Sample space

10. In abstract algebra, a module S over a ring R is called _____ or irreducible if it is not the zero module 0 and if its only submodules are 0 and S. Understanding the _____ modules over a ring is usually helpful because these modules form the 'building blocks' of all other modules in a certain sense.

Abelian groups are the same as Z-modules.

a. Simple b. Harmonic series
c. Basis d. Derivation

11. In mathematics, _____ and undefined are used to explain whether or not expressions have meaningful, sensible, and unambiguous values. Not all branches of mathematics come to the same conclusion.

The following expressions are undefined in all contexts, but remarks in the analysis section may apply.

a. Plugging in b. Toy model
c. LHS d. Defined

12. In game theory, an _____ is a set of moves or strategies taken by the players, or their payoffs resulting from the actions or strategies taken by all players. The two are complementary in that given knowledge of the set of strategies of all players, the final state of the game is known, as are any relevant payoffs. In a game where chance or a random event is involved, the _____ is not known from only the set of strategies, but is only realized when the random even are realized.

a. Autonomous system b. Algebraic
c. Equaliser d. Outcome

Chapter 8. Probability

13. The mathematical concept of a _____ expresses the intuitive idea of deterministic dependence between two quantities, one of which is viewed as primary and the other as secondary. A _____ then is a way to associate a unique output for each input of a specified type, for example, a real number or an element of a given set.
    a. Coherent
    b. Grill
    c. Going up
    d. Function

14. _____ or experimental probability, is the ratio of the number favorable outcomes to the total number of trials, not in a sample space but in an actual sequence of experiments. In a more general sense, _____ estimates probabilities from experience and observation. The phrase a posteriori probability has also been used an alternative to _____ or relative frequency.
    a. A Mathematical Theory of Communication
    b. A posteriori
    c. A chemical equation
    d. Empirical probability

15. In statistics the _____ of an event i is the number n_i of times the event occurred in the experiment or the study. These frequencies are often graphically represented in histograms.

We speak of absolute frequencies, when the counts n_i themselves are given and of

$$f_i = \frac{n_i}{N} = \frac{n_i}{\sum_i n_i}$$

Taking the f_i for all i and tabulating or plotting them leads to a _____ distribution.

   a. Robinson-Dadson curves
   b. Subharmonic
   c. Digital room correction
   d. Frequency

16. _____ is the interpretation of probability that defines an event's probability as the limit of its relative frequency in a large number of trials. The development of the frequentist account was motivated by the problems and paradoxes of the previously dominant viewpoint, the classical interpretation. The shift from the classical view to the frequentist view represents a paradigm shift in the progression of statistical thought.
    a. 120-cell
    b. 1-center problem
    c. Probabilistic proposition
    d. Frequency Probability

17. In mathematics, the _____ of two sets A and B is the set that contains all elements of A that also belong to B, but no other elements.

For explanation of the symbols used in this article, refer to the table of mathematical symbols.

The _____ of A and B

The _____ of A and B is written 'A ∩ B'. Formally:

   x is an element of A ∩ B if and only if
   - x is an element of A and
   - x is an element of B.
   For example:
   - The _____ of the sets {1, 2, 3} and {2, 3, 4} is {2, 3}.
   - The number 9 is not in the _____ of the set of prime numbers {2, 3, 5, 7, 11, …} and the set of odd numbers {1, 3, 5, 7, 9, 11, …}.

If the _____ of two sets A and B is empty, that is they have no elements in common, then they are said to be disjoint, denoted: A ∩ B = Ø. For example the sets {1, 2} and {3, 4} are disjoint, written
{1, 2} ∩ {3, 4} = Ø.

   a. Intersection   b. Erlang
   c. Order   d. Advice

18.   In set theory, the term _____ refers to a set operation used in the convergence of set elements to form a resultant set containing the elements of both sets. As a simple example, a _____ of two disjoint sets, which do not have elements in common results in a set containing all elements from both sets. A Venn diagram representing the _____ of sets A and B.
   a. Union   b. Event
   c. UES   d. Introduction

19.   In simple terms, two events are _____ if they cannot occur at the same time.

In logic, two _____ propositions are propositions that logically cannot both be true. To say that more than two propositions are _____ may, depending on context mean that no two of them can both be true, or only that they cannot all be true.

   a. Philosophy   b. Determinism
   c. Philosophy of mathematics   d. Mutually exclusive

20.   In discrete mathematics and predominantly in set theory, a _____ is a concept used in comparisons of sets to refer to the unique values of one set in relation to another. The terms 'absolute' and 'relative' _____ refer to more specific applications of the concept, with universal _____s referring to elements unique to the universal set and the latter referring to the unique elements of one set in relation to another. In this image, the universal set is represented by the border of the image, and the set A as a disc.
   a. Complement   b. Kernel
   c. Huge   d. Derivative algebra

21.   In engineering and manufacturing, _____ is involved in developing systems to ensure products or services are designed and produced to meet or exceed customer requirements or SLA's. Genetic algorithms are search techniques, used in computing to find exact or approximate solutions to optimization and search problems.

Chapter 8. Probability

Alternative _____ procedures can be applied on a process to test statistically the null hypothesis, that the process is in control, against the alternative, that the process is out of control.

a. 1-center problem
b. 120-cell
c. Statistical process control
d. Quality control

22. In probability theory and statistics the _____ in favour of an event or a proposition are the quantity p /, where p is the probability of the event or proposition. The _____ against the same event are / p. For example, if you chose a random day of the week, then the _____ that you would choose a Sunday would be 1/6, not 1/7.

a. Event
b. Estimation of covariance matrices
c. Odds
d. Anscombe transform

23. A _____ is a structured activity, usually undertaken for enjoyment and sometimes also used as an educational tool. _____s are distinct from work, which is usually carried out for remuneration, and from art, which is more concerned with the expression of ideas. However, the distinction is not clear-cut, and many _____s are also considered to be work (such as professional players of spectator sports/_____s) or art (such as jigsaw puzzles or _____s involving an artistic layout such as Mah-jongg solitaire.)

a. 2-3 heap
b. 1-center problem
c. 120-cell
d. Game

24. The _____ is a theorem in probability that describes the long-term stability of the mean of a random variable. Given a random variable with a finite expected value, if its values are repeatedly sampled, as the number of these observations increases, their mean will tend to approach and stay close to the expected value.

The LLN can easily be illustrated using the rolls of a die.

a. Random field
b. Law of large numbers
c. Point process
d. Graphical model

25. A _____ is a software program that facilitates symbolic mathematics. The core functionality of a CAS is manipulation of mathematical expressions in symbolic form.

The symbolic manipulations supported typically include

- simplification to the smallest possible expression or some standard form, including automatic simplification with assumptions and simplification with constraints
- substitution of symbolic, functors or numeric values for expressions
- change of form of expressions: expanding products and powers, partial and full factorization, rewriting as partial fractions, constraint satisfaction, rewriting trigonometric functions as exponentials, etc.
- partial and total differentiation
- symbolic constrained and unconstrained global optimization
- solution of linear and some non-linear equations over various domains
- solution of some differential and difference equations
- taking some limits
- some indefinite and definite integration, including multidimensional integrals
- integral transforms
- arbitrary-precision numeric operations
- Series operations such as expansion, summation and products
- matrix operations including products, inverses, etc.
- display of mathematical expressions in two-dimensional mathematical form, often using typesetting systems similar to TeX
- add-ons for use in applied mathematics such as physics packages for physical computation
- plotting graphs and parametric plots of functions in two and three dimensions, and animating them
- APIs for linking it on an external program such as a database, or using in a programming language to use the _____
- drawing charts and diagrams
- string manipulation such as matching and searching
- statistical computation
- Theorem proving and verification
- graphic production and editing such as CGI and signal processing as image processing
- sound synthesis

Many also include a programming language, allowing users to implement their own algorithms.

Some _____s focus on a specific area of application; these are typically developed in academia and are free.

a. 1-center problem
c. 120-cell
b. 2-3 heap
d. Computer algebra system

26. In mathematics and physics, there are a _____ number of topics named in honor of Leonhard Euler . As well, many of these topics include their own unique function, equation, formula, identity, number, or other mathematical entity. Unfortunately however, many of these entities have been given simple names like Euler's function, Euler's equation, and Euler's formula, which are further confused by variations of the 'Euler'-prefix Overall though, Euler's work touched upon so many fields that he is often the earliest written reference on a given matter.

a. List of trigonometry topics
b. List of integrals of logarithmic functions
c. List of mathematical knots and links
d. Large

27. The _____ governs the differentiation of products of differentiable functions.
a. Reciprocal Rule
b. 120-cell
c. Product rule
d. 1-center problem

28. In mathematics, a _____ is a statement that can be proved on the basis of explicitly stated or previously agreed assumptions.
a. Boolean function
b. Logical value
c. Disjunction introduction
d. Theorem

29. In set theory, a _____ is a partially ordered set such that for each $t \in T$, the set $\{s \in T : s < t\}$ is well-ordered by the relation <. For each $t \in T$, the order type of $\{s \in T : s < t\}$ is called the height of t. The height of T itself is the least ordinal greater than the height of each element of T.
a. Transitive reduction
b. Set-theoretic topology
c. Definable numbers
d. Tree

30. A _____ is the counterpart to a deterministic process in probability theory. Instead of dealing with only one possible 'reality' of how the process might evolve under time, in a stochastic or random process there is some indeterminacy in its future evolution described by probability distributions. This means that even if the initial condition is known, there are many possibilities the process might go to, but some paths are more probable and others less.
a. Stochastic simulation
b. Stochastic process
c. Fractional Brownian motion
d. Mixing time

31. In graph theory, an _____ or stable set is a set of vertices in a graph no two of which are adjacent. That is, it is a set V of vertices such that for every two vertices in V, there is no edge connecting the two. Equivalently, each edge in the graph has at most one endpoint in V.
a. Eulerian path
b. Independent set
c. Instant Insanity
d. Isomorphism of graphs

32. In probability theory and statistics, a _____ identifies either the probability of each value of an unidentified random variable, or the probability of the value falling within a particular interval. The probability function describes the range of possible values that a random variable can attain and the probability that the value of the random variable is within any subset of that range.

When the random variable takes values in the set of real numbers, the _____ is completely described by the cumulative distribution function, whose value at each real x is the probability that the random variable is smaller than or equal to x.

a. Normal distribution
b. Z-test
c. Statistical graphics
d. Probability distribution

Chapter 8. Probability

33. In mathematics, _____ are used in the study of chance and probability. They were developed to assist in the analysis of games of chance, stochastic events, and the results of scientific experiments by capturing only the mathematical properties necessary to answer probabilistic questions. Further formalizations have firmly grounded the entity in the theoretical domains of mathematics by making use of measure theory.
   a. Median polish
   b. Random variables
   c. Statistical dispersion
   d. Statistics

34. In differential geometry, a discipline within mathematics, a _____ is a subset of the tangent bundle of a manifold satisfying certain properties. _____s are used to build up notions of integrability, and specifically of a foliation of a manifold
   a. Discontinuity
   b. Distribution
   c. Constraint
   d. Coherence

35. In probability theory and statistics, the _____ of a random variable is the integral of the random variable with respect to its probability measure. For discrete random variables this is equivalent to the probability-weighted sum of the possible values, and for continuous random variables with a density function it is the probability density -weighted integral of the possible values.

    The _____ may be intuitively understood by the law of large numbers: The _____, when it exists, is almost surely the limit of the sample mean as sample size grows to infinity.

   a. Infinitely divisible distribution
   b. Illustration
   c. Event
   d. Expected value

36. In statistics, a _____ is a graphical display of tabulated frequencies, shown as bars. It shows what proportion of cases fall into each of several categories. A _____ differs from a bar chart in that it is the area of the bar that denotes the value, not the height as in bar charts, a crucial distinction when the categories are not of uniform width.
   a. First-hitting-time models
   b. Standardized moment
   c. Probability distribution
   d. Histogram

37. _____ can be regarded as an outcome of mental processes leading to the selection of a course of action among several alternatives. Every _____ process produces a final choice. The output can be an action or an opinion of choice.
   a. 1-center problem
   b. 2-3 heap
   c. 120-cell
   d. Decision making

38. In mathematics, hyperbolic n-space, denoted H^n, is the maximally symmetric, simply connected, n-dimensional Riemannian manifold with constant sectional curvature −1. _____ is the principal example of a space exhibiting hyperbolic geometry. It can be thought of as the negative-curvature analogue of the n-sphere.
   a. Hyperbolic geometry
   b. Horocycle
   c. Margulis lemma
   d. Hyperbolic space

Chapter 9. Markov Chains

1. In mathematics, a _____, named after Andrey Markov, is a stochastic process with the Markov property. Having the Markov property means that, given the present state, future states are independent of the past states. In other words, the description of the present state fully captures all the information that could influence the future evolution of the process. Future states will be reached through a probabilistic process instead of a deterministic one.
   a. Variance-to-mean ratio
   b. Possibility theory
   c. Law of Truly Large Numbers
   d. Markov chain

2. A _____ is the counterpart to a deterministic process in probability theory. Instead of dealing with only one possible 'reality' of how the process might evolve under time, in a stochastic or random process there is some indeterminacy in its future evolution described by probability distributions. This means that even if the initial condition is known, there are many possibilities the process might go to, but some paths are more probable and others less.
   a. Mixing time
   b. Stochastic simulation
   c. Fractional Brownian motion
   d. Stochastic process

3. A _____ is a 2D geometric symbolic representation of information according to some visualization technique. Sometimes, the technique uses a 3D visualization which is then projected onto the 2D surface. The word graph is sometimes used as a synonym for _____.
   a. 1-center problem
   b. 120-cell
   c. 2-3 heap
   d. Diagram

4. In mathematics, a _____ is a rectangular table of elements, which may be numbers or, more generally, any abstract quantities that can be added and multiplied. Matrices are used to describe linear equations, keep track of the coefficients of linear transformations and to record data that depend on multiple parameters. Matrices are described by the field of _____ theory.
   a. Coherent
   b. Compression
   c. Double counting
   d. Matrix

5. _____ is the likelihood or chance that something is the case or will happen. Theoretical _____ is used extensively in areas such as statistics, mathematics, science and philosophy to draw conclusions about the likelihood of potential events and the underlying mechanics of complex systems.

   The word _____ does not have a consistent direct definition.

   a. Discrete random variable
   b. Standardized moment
   c. Probability
   d. Statistical significance

6. In differential geometry, a discipline within mathematics, a _____ is a subset of the tangent bundle of a manifold satisfying certain properties. _____s are used to build up notions of integrability, and specifically of a foliation of a manifold
   a. Distribution
   b. Discontinuity
   c. Constraint
   d. Coherence

7. In mathematics, a stochastic matrix, probability matrix, or _____ is used to describe the transitions of a Markov chain. It has found use in probability theory, statistics and linear algebra, as well as computer science. There are several different definitions and types of stochastic matrices;

A right stochastic matrix is a square matrix each of whose rows consists of nonnegative real numbers, with each row summing to 1.

a. Hessenberg matrix
c. Sylvester matrix
b. Transition matrix
d. Pick matrix

8. In mathematics, _____ and undefined are used to explain whether or not expressions have meaningful, sensible, and unambiguous values. Not all branches of mathematics come to the same conclusion.

The following expressions are undefined in all contexts, but remarks in the analysis section may apply.

a. Plugging in
c. LHS
b. Toy model
d. Defined

9. In commutative algebra, the notions of an element _____ over a ring, and of an _____ extension of rings, are a generalization of the notions in field theory of an element being algebraic over a field, and of an algebraic extension of fields.

The special case of greatest interest in number theory is that of complex numbers _____ over the ring of integers Z.

The term ring will be understood to mean commutative ring with a unit.

a. Antidifferentiation
c. Arc length
b. Integral test for convergence
d. Integral

10. In mathematics, hyperbolic n-space, denoted H^n, is the maximally symmetric, simply connected, n-dimensional Riemannian manifold with constant sectional curvature −1. _____ is the principal example of a space exhibiting hyperbolic geometry. It can be thought of as the negative-curvature analogue of the n-sphere.

a. Hyperbolic space
c. Hyperbolic geometry
b. Horocycle
d. Margulis lemma

11. _____ is a branch of mathematics which focuses on the study of matrices. Initially a sub-branch of linear algebra, it has grown to cover subjects related to graph theory, algebra, combinatorics, and statistics as well.

The term matrix was first coined in 1848 by J.J. Sylvester as a name of an array of numbers.

a. Semi-simple operators
c. Segre classification
b. Pairing
d. Matrix theory

12. _____ Any process by which a specified characteristic usually amplitude of the output of a device is prevented from exceeding a predetermined value.

a. Limiting
c. Parametric continuity
b. Logical equivalence
d. Notation

Chapter 9. Markov Chains

13. A _____ is a software program that facilitates symbolic mathematics. The core functionality of a CAS is manipulation of mathematical expressions in symbolic form.

The symbolic manipulations supported typically include

- simplification to the smallest possible expression or some standard form, including automatic simplification with assumptions and simplification with constraints
- substitution of symbolic, functors or numeric values for expressions
- change of form of expressions: expanding products and powers, partial and full factorization, rewriting as partial fractions, constraint satisfaction, rewriting trigonometric functions as exponentials, etc.
- partial and total differentiation
- symbolic constrained and unconstrained global optimization
- solution of linear and some non-linear equations over various domains
- solution of some differential and difference equations
- taking some limits
- some indefinite and definite integration, including multidimensional integrals
- integral transforms
- arbitrary-precision numeric operations
- Series operations such as expansion, summation and products
- matrix operations including products, inverses, etc.
- display of mathematical expressions in two-dimensional mathematical form, often using typesetting systems similar to TeX
- add-ons for use in applied mathematics such as physics packages for physical computation
- plotting graphs and parametric plots of functions in two and three dimensions, and animating them
- APIs for linking it on an external program such as a database, or using in a programming language to use the _____
- drawing charts and diagrams
- string manipulation such as matching and searching
- statistical computation
- Theorem proving and verification
- graphic production and editing such as CGI and signal processing as image processing
- sound synthesis

Many also include a programming language, allowing users to implement their own algorithms.

Some _____s focus on a specific area of application; these are typically developed in academia and are free.

a. Computer algebra system
c. 2-3 heap
b. 120-cell
d. 1-center problem

14. A _____ is a device for performing mathematical calculations, distinguished from a computer by having a limited problem solving ability and an interface optimized for interactive calculation rather than programming. _____s can be hardware or software, and mechanical or electronic, and are often built into devices such as PDAs or mobile phones.

Modern electronic _____ s are generally small, digital, and usually inexpensive.

a. Calculator
b. 2-3 heap
c. 1-center problem
d. 120-cell

15. A _____ typically refers to a class of handheld calculators that are capable of plotting graphs, solving simultaneous equations, and performing numerous other tasks with variables. Most popular _____ s are also programmable, allowing the user to create customized programs, typically for scientific/engineering and education applications. Due to their large displays intended for graphing, they can also accommodate several lines of text and calculations at a time.

a. Graphing calculator
b. Support vector machines
c. Genus
d. Bump mapping

16. In simple terms, two events are _____ if they cannot occur at the same time.

In logic, two _____ propositions are propositions that logically cannot both be true. To say that more than two propositions are _____ may, depending on context mean that no two of them can both be true, or only that they cannot all be true.

a. Determinism
b. Mutually exclusive
c. Philosophy of mathematics
d. Philosophy

17. In probability theory, an _____ is a set of outcomes to which a probability is assigned. Typically, when the sample space is finite, any subset of the sample space is an _____. However, this approach does not work well in cases where the sample space is infinite, most notably when the outcome is a real number.

a. Equaliser
b. Information set
c. Audio compression
d. Event

18. _____, also sometimes known as standard form or as exponential notation, is a way of writing numbers that accommodates values too large or small to be conveniently written in standard decimal notation. _____ has a number of useful properties and is often favored by scientists, mathematicians and engineers, who work with such numbers.

In _____, numbers are written in the form:

$$a \times 10^b$$

a. Scientific notation
b. Leading zero
c. 1-center problem
d. Radix point

19. In classical differential geometry, _____ refers to the simple idea of rolling one smooth surface over another in Euclidean space. For example, the tangent plane to a surface at a point can be rolled around the surface to obtain the tangent-plane at other points.

The tangential contact between the surfaces being rolled over one another provides a relation between points on the two surfaces.

a. Double counting
b. FISH
c. Blinding
d. Development

20. _____ is a legal term (in some jurisdictions, notably in the USA, United Kingdom, Canada, and Australia) that encompasses land along with anything permanently affixed to the land, such as buildings, specifically property that is stationary, or fixed in location. _____ law is the body of regulations and legal codes which pertain to such matters under a particular jurisdiction. _____ is often considered synonymous with real property (also sometimes called realty), in contrast with personal property (also sometimes called chattel or personalty under chattel law or personal property law.)

a. 120-cell
b. 1-center problem
c. Home equity
d. Real estate

21. In mathematics, a _____ is a statement that can be proved on the basis of explicitly stated or previously agreed assumptions.

a. Disjunction introduction
b. Boolean function
c. Theorem
d. Logical value

Chapter 10. Limits and the Derivative

1. In cryptography, _____ is a pseudorandom number generator and a stream cipher designed by Robert Jenkins to be cryptographically secure. The name is an acronym for Indirection, Shift, Accumulate, Add, and Count.

The _____ algorithm has similarities with RC4.

   a. Imputation
   c. Order
   b. Introduction
   d. Isaac

2. _____ was a German polymath who wrote primarily in Latin and French.

He occupies an equally grand place in both the history of philosophy and the history of mathematics. He invented infinitesimal calculus independently of Newton, and his notation is the one in general use since then.

   a. Raymond Merrill Smullyan
   c. Michel Rolle
   b. Harry Hinsley
   d. Gottfried Wilhelm Leibniz

3. The _____ (symbol: N) is the SI derived unit of force, named after Isaac _____ in recognition of his work on classical mechanics.

The _____ is the unit of force derived in the SI system; it is equal to the amount of force required to accelerate a mass of one kilogram at a rate of one meter per second per second. Algebraically:

$$1\ \text{N} = 1\ \frac{\text{kg} \cdot \text{m}}{\text{s}^2}.$$

- 1 N is the force of Earth's gravity on an object with a mass of about 102 g ($1/_{9.8}$ kg) (such as a small apple.)
- On Earth's surface, a mass of 1 kg exerts a force of approximately 9.80665 N [down] (or 1 kgf.) The approximation of 1 kg corresponding to 10 N is sometimes used as a rule of thumb in everyday life and in engineering.
- The force of Earth's gravity on a human being with a mass of 70 kg is approximately 687 N.
- The dot product of force and distance is mechanical work. Thus, in SI units, a force of 1 N exerted over a distance of 1 m is 1 N·m of work. The Work-Energy Theorem states that the work done on a body is equal to the change in energy of the body. 1 N·m = 1 J (joule), the SI unit of energy.
- It is common to see forces expressed in kilonewtons or kN, where 1 kN = 1 000 N.

   a. 120-cell
   c. 2-3 heap
   b. 1-center problem
   d. Newton

4. In vascular plants, the _____ is the organ of a plant body that typically lies below the surface of the soil. This is not always the case, however, since a _____ can also be aerial (that is, growing above the ground) or aerating (that is, growing up above the ground or especially above water.) Furthermore, a stem normally occurring below ground is not exceptional either

Chapter 10. Limits and the Derivative

    a. Root
    c. 2-3 heap
    b. 120-cell
    d. 1-center problem

5. In mathematics, a _____ of a number x is a number r such that r^2 = x, or, in other words, a number r whose square is x. Every non-negative real number x has a unique non-negative _____, called the principal _____, which is denoted with a radical symbol as $\sqrt{x}$, or, using exponent notation, as $x^{1/2}$. For example, the principal _____ of 9 is 3, denoted $\sqrt{9}$ = 3, because 3^2 = 3 × 3 = 9.

    a. Square root
    c. Double exponential
    b. Multiplicative inverse
    d. Hyperbolic functions

6. The mathematical concept of a _____ expresses the intuitive idea of deterministic dependence between two quantities, one of which is viewed as primary and the other as secondary. A _____ then is a way to associate a unique output for each input of a specified type, for example, a real number or an element of a given set.

    a. Coherent
    c. Going up
    b. Grill
    d. Function

7. In mathematics, the concept of a '_____' is used to describe the behavior of a function as its argument or input either 'gets close' to some point, or as the argument becomes arbitrarily large; or the behavior of a sequence's elements as their index increases indefinitely. _____s are used in calculus and other branches of mathematical analysis to define derivatives and continuity.

In formulas, _____ is usually abbreviated as lim.

    a. Contact
    c. Copula
    b. Limit
    d. Duality

8. In mathematics, a _____ of a set S in a topological space X is a point x in X that can be 'approximated' by points of S other than x itself. This concept profitably generalizes the notion of a limit and is the underpinning of concepts such as closed set and topological closure. Indeed, a set is closed if and only if it contains all of its _____s, and the topological closure operation can be thought of as an operation that enriches a set by adding its _____s.

    a. Limit point
    c. 2-3 heap
    b. 1-center problem
    d. 120-cell

9. In mathematics, _____ and undefined are used to explain whether or not expressions have meaningful, sensible, and unambiguous values. Not all branches of mathematics come to the same conclusion.

The following expressions are undefined in all contexts, but remarks in the analysis section may apply.

    a. LHS
    c. Plugging in
    b. Toy model
    d. Defined

10. In mathematics, the _____ of a real number is its numerical value without regard to its sign. So, for example, 3 is the _____ of both 3 and −3.

The _____ of a number a is denoted by $|a|$.

Generalizations of the _____ for real numbers occur in a wide variety of mathematical settings.

a. A Mathematical Theory of Communication
b. A chemical equation
c. Area hyperbolic functions
d. Absolute value

11. In calculus, a _____ is either of the two limits of a function f

$$\lim_{x \to a^+} f(x) \text{ or } \lim_{x \downarrow a} f(x)$$

for the limit as x approaches a from above, and similarly

$$\lim_{x \to a^-} f(x) \text{ or } \lim_{x \uparrow a} f(x)$$

for the limit as x approaches a from below.

The two _____s exist and are equal if and only if the limit of f

a. Archimedes' use of infinitesimals
b. Uniform convergence
c. Infinite series
d. One-sided limit

12. In abstract algebra, a field extension L /K is called _____ if every element of L is _____ over K. Field extensions which are not _____.

For example, the field extension R/Q, that is the field of real numbers as an extension of the field of rational numbers, is transcendental, while the field extensions C/R and Q

a. Ideal
b. Identity
c. Echo
d. Algebraic

13. In mathematics, a _____ is an expression constructed from variables and constants, using the operations of addition, subtraction, multiplication, and constant non-negative whole number exponents. For example, $x^2 - 4x + 7$ is a _____, but $x^2 - 4/x + 7x^{3/2}$ is not, because its second term involves division by the variable x and also because its third term contains an exponent that is not a whole number.

_____s are one of the most important concepts in algebra and throughout mathematics and science.

a. Polynomial
b. Group extension
c. Coimage
d. Semifield

Chapter 10. Limits and the Derivative

14. In mathematics, a _____ is any function which can be written as the ratio of two polynomial functions. _____ of degree 2 :

$$y = \frac{x^2 - 3x - 2}{x^2 - 4}$$

In the case of one variable, x, a _____ is a function of the form

$$f(x) = \frac{P(x)}{Q(x)}$$

where P and Q are polynomial function in x and Q is not the zero polynomial. The domain of f is the set of all points x for which the denominator Q

a. Legendre rational functions
b. 1-center problem
c. 120-cell
d. Rational function

15. In mathematics, more precisely in algebra, an _____ is a quantity that is not known, and cannot be solved for. An _____ is different from a variable, which is solvable, at least conditionally, from a given equation or set of equations. To make this distinction in an example, compare these two situations.

a. Algebraic function
b. Immanant of a matrix
c. Algebraic solution
d. Indeterminate

16. In calculus and other branches of mathematical analysis, an _____ is an algebraic expression obtained in the context of limits. Limits involving algebraic operations are often performed by replacing subexpressions by their limits; if the expression obtained after this substitution does not give enough information to determine the original limit, it is known as an _____. The _____s include 0^0, 0/0, 1^∞, $\infty - \infty$, ∞/∞, $0 \times \infty$, and ∞^0.

a. Exponential function can be characterized
b. Uniformly absolutely continuous
c. Improper integral
d. Indeterminate form

17. In mathematics, a _____ is the end result of a division problem. It can also be expressed as the number of times the divisor divides into the dividend.

a. Marginal cost
b. Quotient
c. Limiting
d. Notation

18. _____ is a fundamental construction of differential calculus and admits many possible generalizations within the fields of mathematical analysis, combinatorics, algebra, and geometry.

In real, complex, and functional analysis, _____s are generalized to functions of several real or complex variables and functions between topological vector spaces. An important case is the variational _____ in the calculus of variations.

a. Lin-Tsien equation
b. Metric derivative
c. Functional derivative
d. Derivative

Chapter 10. Limits and the Derivative

19. In mathematics, an _____, or central tendency of a data set refers to a measure of the 'middle' or 'expected' value of the data set. There are many different descriptive statistics that can be chosen as a measurement of the central tendency of the data items.

An _____ is a single value that is meant to typify a list of values.

a. A Mathematical Theory of Communication
b. A chemical equation
c. A posteriori
d. Average

20. In set theory, the term _____ refers to a set operation used in the convergence of set elements to form a resultant set containing the elements of both sets. As a simple example, a _____ of two disjoint sets, which do not have elements in common results in a set containing all elements from both sets. A Venn diagram representing the _____ of sets A and B.

a. UES
b. Introduction
c. Union
d. Event

21. In probability theory, a probability distribution is called _____ if its cumulative distribution function is _____. That is equivalent to saying that for random variables X with the distribution in question, Pr[X = a] = 0 for all real numbers a. If the distribution of X is _____ then X is called a _____ random variable.

a. Conull set
b. Concatenated codes
c. Continuous
d. Continuous phase modulation

22. In mathematics, a _____ is a function for which, intuitively, small changes in the input result in small changes in the output. Otherwise, a function is said to be discontinuous. A _____ with a continuous inverse function is called bicontinuous.

a. Contraction mapping
b. Beth numbers
c. Charles's Law
d. Continuous function

23. In mathematics, a _____ is a set of real numbers with the property that any number that lies between two numbers in the set is also included in the set. For example, the set of all numbers x satisfying $0 \leq x \leq 1$ is an _____ which contains 0 and 1, as well as all numbers between them. Other examples of _____s are the set of all real numbers $\mathbb{R}$, the set of all positive real numbers, and the empty set.

a. Annihilator
b. Ideal
c. Order
d. Interval

24. In mathematics, a _____ is a function whose values do not vary and thus are constant. For example, if we have the function f→ B is a _____ iff f

a. Squeeze mapping
b. Point reflection
c. Linear operator
d. Constant function

25. The _____ are the set of numbers consisting of the natural numbers including 0 and their negatives. They are numbers that can be written without a fractional or decimal component, and fall within the set {... −2, −1, 0, 1, 2, ...}.

a. A chemical equation
b. A posteriori
c. A Mathematical Theory of Communication
d. Integers

26. In number theory, a _____ of a positive integer n is a way of writing n as a sum of positive integers. Two sums which only differ in the order of their summands are considered to be the same _____; if order matters then the sum becomes a composition. A summand in a _____ is also called a part.
   a. Congruent
   b. Distribution
   c. Partition
   d. Derivative algebra

27. In mathematics, an _____ is a statement about the relative size or order of two objects, or about whether they are the same or not

   - The notation a < b means that a is less than b.
   - The notation a > b means that a is greater than b.
   - The notation a ≠ b means that a is not equal to b, but does not say that one is bigger than the other or even that they can be compared in size.

In all these cases, a is not equal to b, hence, '_____'.

These relations are known as strict _____

   - The notation a ≤ b means that a is less than or equal to b;
   - The notation a ≥ b means that a is greater than or equal to b;

An additional use of the notation is to show that one quantity is much greater than another, normally by several orders of magnitude.

   - The notation a << b means that a is much less than b.
   - The notation a >> b means that a is much greater than b.

If the sense of the _____ is the same for all values of the variables for which its members are defined, then the _____ is called an 'absolute' or 'unconditional' _____. If the sense of an _____ holds only for certain values of the variables involved, but is reversed or destroyed for other values of the variables, it is called a conditional _____.

An _____ may appear unsolvable because it only states whether a number is larger or smaller than another number; but it is possible to apply the same operations for equalities to inequalities. For example, to find x for the _____ 10x > 23 one would divide 23 by 10.

   a. Inequality
   b. A posteriori
   c. A Mathematical Theory of Communication
   d. A chemical equation

28. An _____ of a real-valued function y = f(x) is a curve which describes the behavior of f as either x or y tends to infinity.

In other words, as one moves along the graph of f(x) in some direction, the distance between it and the _____ eventually becomes smaller than any distance that one may specify.

If a curve A has the curve B as an _____, one says that A is asymptotic to B. Similarly B is asymptotic to A, so A and B are called asymptotic.

a. Asymptote
c. Infinite product

b. Improper integral
d. Isoperimetric dimension

29. _____ is the state of being greater than any finite number, however large.
a. Interval notation
c. A Mathematical Theory of Communication

b. Implicit differentiation
d. Infinity

30. Suppose f is a function. Then the line y = a is a _____ for f if

$$\lim_{x \to \infty} f(x) = a \text{ or } \lim_{x \to -\infty} f(x) = a.$$

Intuitively, this means that f(x) can be made as close as desired to a by making x big enough. How big is big enough depends on how close one wishes to make f(x) to a.

a. 2-3 heap
c. 1-center problem

b. Horizontal asymptote
d. 120-cell

31. The _____ program is a directory search utility on Unix-like platforms. It searches through one or more directory trees of a filesystem, locating files based on some user-specified criteria. By default, _____ returns all files below the current working directory.

a. 2-3 heap
c. 120-cell

b. 1-center problem
d. Find

32. _____ of an object is its speed in a particular direction.
a. Velocity
c. Discontinuity

b. Maxima
d. Rolle's Theorem

33. _____ is a term in mathematics. It can refer to:

- a _____ line, in geometry
- the trigonometric function called _____
- the _____ method, a root-finding algorithm in numerical analysis

a. Large set
c. Secant

b. Solvable
d. Separable

34. _____ is used to describe the steepness, incline, gradient, or grade of a straight line. A higher _____ value indicates a steeper incline. The _____ is defined as the ratio of the 'rise' divided by the 'run' between two points on a line, or in other words, the ratio of the altitude change to the horizontal distance between any two points on the line.

a. Number line	b. Slope
c. Point plotting	d. Cognitively Guided Instruction

35. In trigonometry, the _____ is a function defined as tan x = $^{sin\ x}/_{cos\ x}$. The function is so-named because it can be defined as the length of a certain segment of a _____ (in the geometric sense) to the unit circle. In plane geometry, a line is _____ to a curve, at some point, if both line and curve pass through the point with the same direction.

a. Projective connection	b. Tangent
c. Conformal geometry	d. Hopf conjectures

36. In geometry, the _____ to a curve at a given point is the straight line that 'just touches' the curve at that point. As it passes through the point of tangency, the _____ is 'going in the same direction' as the curve, and in this sense it is the best straight-line approximation to the curve at that point. The same definition applies to space curves and curves in n-dimensional Euclidean space.

a. Darboux frame	b. Chern-Weil theory
c. Four-vertex theorem	d. Tangent line

37. This article will state and prove the _____ for differentiation, and then use it to prove these two formulas.

The _____ for differentiation states that for every natural number n, the derivative of $f(x) = x^n$ is $f'(x) = nx^{n-1}$, that is,

$$(x^n)' = nx^{n-1}.$$

The _____ for integration

$$\int x^n\, dx = \frac{x^{n+1}}{n+1} + C$$

for natural n is then an easy consequence. One just needs to take the derivative of this equality and use the _____ and linearity of differentiation on the right-hand side.

a. Periodic function	b. Standard part function
c. Functional integration	d. Power rule

38. Suppose that φ : M → N is a smooth map between smooth manifolds; then the _____ of φ at a point x is, in some sense, the best linear approximation of φ near x. It can be viewed as generalization of the total derivative of ordinary calculus. Explicitly, it is a linear map from the tangent space of M at x to the tangent space of N at φ

a. Concurrent	b. Differential
c. Grill	d. Boundary

39. _____s is concerned with the tasks of developing and applying quantitative or statistical methods to the study and elucidation of economic principles. _____s combines economic theory with statistics to analyze and test economic relationships. Theoretical _____s considers questions about the statistical properties of estimators and tests, while applied _____s is concerned with the application of _____ methods to assess economic theories.

a. A Mathematical Theory of Communication
b. Economic
c. A chemical equation
d. Econometric

40. An _____ is an increase of some amount, either fixed or variable. For example one's salary may have a fixed annual _____ or one based on a percentage of its current value. A decrease is called a decrement.
a. A posteriori
b. A chemical equation
c. A Mathematical Theory of Communication
d. Increment

41. In economics, business, retail, and accounting, a _____ is the value of money that has been used up to produce something, and hence is not available for use anymore. In business, the _____ may be one of acquisition, in which case the amount of money expended to acquire it is counted as _____. In this case, money is the input that is gone in order to acquire the thing.
a. Cost
b. 1-center problem
c. 120-cell
d. 2-3 heap

42. _____s is the social science that studies the production, distribution, and consumption of goods and services.

The term _____s comes from the Ancient Greek οá¼°κονομῑα (oikonomia, 'management of a household, administration') from οá¼¶κος (oikos, 'house') + vÏŒμος (nomos, 'custom' or 'law'), hence 'rules of the house(hold)'.

Current _____ models developed out of the broader field of political economy in the late 19th century, owing to a desire to use an empirical approach more akin to the physical sciences.

a. Experimental economics
b. A Mathematical Theory of Communication
c. A chemical equation
d. Economic

43. _____ is the change in total cost that arises when the quantity produced changes by one unit.
a. Notation
b. Differential Algebra
c. Limiting
d. Marginal cost

44. In microeconomics, _____ is the term used to refer to total when marginal cost is subtracted from marginal revenue. Under the marginal approach to profit maximization, to maximize profits, a firm should continue to produce a good until _____ is zero. Profit Maximization - The Marginal Approach

{{Economics-stub}}

a. 2-3 heap
b. 120-cell
c. 1-center problem
d. Marginal profit

45. In economics, the cross elasticity of demand and _____ measures the responsiveness of the quantity demanded of a good to a change in the price of another good.

It is measured as the percentage change in quantity demanded for the first good that occurs in response to a percentage change in price of the second good. For example, if, in response to a 10% increase in the price of fuel, the quantity of new cars that are fuel inefficient demanded decreased by 20%, the cross elasticity of demand would be -20%/10% = -2.

a. Marginal rate of substitution
b. Cross price elasticity of demand
c. Supply and demand
d. 1-center problem

46. In game theory, a player's _____ in a game is a complete plan of action for whatever situation might arise; this fully determines the player's behaviour. A player's _____ will determine the action the player will take at any stage of the game, for every possible history of play up to that stage.

A _____ profile is a set of strategies for each player which fully specifies all actions in a game.

a. Sir Philip Sidney game
b. Correlated equilibrium
c. Strategy
d. Matching pennies

47. In economics, _____ is equal to total cost divided by the number of goods produced Quantity-Q. It is also equal to the sum of average variable costs total variable costs divided by Q plus average fixed costs total fixed costs divided by Q. _____s may be dependent on the time period considered increasing production may be expensive or impossible in the short term, for example. _____s affect the supply curve and are a fundamental component of supply and demand.

a. Uncertainty quantification
b. Extreme value theorem
c. Average cost
d. Equity

Chapter 11. Additional Derivative Topics

1. In probability theory, a probability distribution is called _____ if its cumulative distribution function is _____. That is equivalent to saying that for random variables X with the distribution in question, Pr[X = a] = 0 for all real numbers a. If the distribution of X is _____ then X is called a _____ random variable.
   a. Conull set
   b. Continuous phase modulation
   c. Concatenated codes
   d. Continuous

2. _____ is the concept of adding accumulated interest back to the principal, so that interest is earned on interest from that moment on. The act of declaring interest to be principal is called compounding. A loan, for example, may have its interest compounded every month: in this case, a loan with $100 principal and 1% interest per month would have a balance of $101 at the end of the first month.
   a. Retained interest
   b. Net interest margin securities
   c. Net interest margin
   d. Compound interest

3. _____ is a fee, paid on borrowed capital. Assets lent include money, shares, consumer goods through hire purchase, major assets such as aircraft, and even entire factories in finance lease arrangements. The _____ is calculated upon the value of the assets in the same manner as upon money.
   a. Interest expense
   b. Interest sensitivity gap
   c. A Mathematical Theory of Communication
   d. Interest

4. _____ is usually defined as the activity of using and developing computer technology, computer hardware and software. It is the computer-specific part of information technology. Computer science (or _____ science) is the study and the science of the theoretical foundations of information and computation and their implementation and application in computer systems.
   a. Computing
   b. Deterministic finite state machine
   c. Parallel Random Access Machine
   d. Probabilistic Turing Machine

5. In mathematics and in the sciences, a _____ (plural: _____e, formulæ or _____s) is a concise way of expressing information symbolically (as in a mathematical or chemical _____), or a general relationship between quantities. One of many famous _____e is Albert Einstein's E = mc^2 (see special relativity

In mathematics, a _____ is a key to solve an equation with variables. For example, the problem of determining the volume of a sphere is one that requires a significant amount of integral calculus to solve.

   a. 2-3 heap
   b. 120-cell
   c. 1-center problem
   d. Formula

6. In computational complexity theory, an algorithm is said to take _____ if the asymptotic upper bound for the time it requires is proportional to the size of the input, which is usually denoted n.

Informally spoken, the running time increases linearly with the size of the input. For example, a procedure that adds up all elements of a list requires time proportional to the length of the list.

   a. Time-constructible function
   b. Truth table reduction
   c. Constructible function
   d. Linear time

7. The _____ is the period of time required for a quantity to double in size or value.

Chapter 11. Additional Derivative Topics

a. Power law
b. Stretched exponential function
c. Zenzizenzizenzic
d. Doubling time

8. _____ is a fundamental construction of differential calculus and admits many possible generalizations within the fields of mathematical analysis, combinatorics, algebra, and geometry.

In real, complex, and functional analysis, _____s are generalized to functions of several real or complex variables and functions between topological vector spaces. An important case is the variational _____ in the calculus of variations.

a. Metric derivative
b. Functional derivative
c. Lin-Tsien equation
d. Derivative

9. The mathematical concept of a _____ expresses the intuitive idea of deterministic dependence between two quantities, one of which is viewed as primary and the other as secondary. A _____ then is a way to associate a unique output for each input of a specified type, for example, a real number or an element of a given set.
a. Grill
b. Going up
c. Function
d. Coherent

10. The function $\log_b(x)$ depends on both b and x, but the term _____ (or logarithmic function) in standard usage refers to a function of the form $\log_b(x)$ in which the base b is fixed and so the only argument is x. Thus there is one _____ for each value of the base b (which must be positive and must differ from 1.) Viewed in this way, the base-b _____ is the inverse function of the exponential function b^x.
a. 120-cell
b. 2-3 heap
c. Logarithm function
d. 1-center problem

11. In mathematics, _____ and undefined are used to explain whether or not expressions have meaningful, sensible, and unambiguous values. Not all branches of mathematics come to the same conclusion.

The following expressions are undefined in all contexts, but remarks in the analysis section may apply.

a. Plugging in
b. Toy model
c. LHS
d. Defined

12. The _____ is a function in mathematics. The application of this function to a value x is written as ex. Equivalently, this can be written in the form e^x, where e is a mathematical constant, the base of the natural logarithm, which equals approximately 2.718281828, and is also known as Euler's number.
a. Exponential function
b. A chemical equation
c. Area hyperbolic functions
d. A Mathematical Theory of Communication

13. In ecology, predation describes a biological interaction where a _____ (an organism that is hunting) feeds on its prey, the organism that is attacked. _____s may or may not kill their prey prior to feeding on them, but the act of predation always results in the death of the prey. The other main category of consumption is detritivory, the consumption of dead organic material (detritus.)

a. 120-cell
b. Prey
c. 1-center problem
d. Predator

14. A _____ is a large fiber or metal rope, used for hauling, lifting or an assembly of two or more insulated electrical conductors, laid up together as an assembly. An optical _____ contains one or more optical fibers in a protective jacket that supports the fibers.

Ropes made of multiple strands of natural fibers such as hemp, sisal, manila, and cotton have been used for millennia for hoisting and hauling.

a. 2-3 heap
b. 1-center problem
c. 120-cell
d. Cable

15. The _____ governs the differentiation of products of differentiable functions.
a. 1-center problem
b. 120-cell
c. Reciprocal Rule
d. Product rule

16. In mathematics, the _____ is an approach to finding a particular solution to certain inhomogeneous ordinary differential equations and recurrence relations. It is closely related to the annihilator method, but instead of using a particular kind of differential operator in order to find the best possible form of the particular solution, a 'guess' is made as to the appropriate form, which is then tested by differentiating the resulting equation. In this sense, the _____ is less formal but more intuitive than the annihilator method.
a. Differential algebraic equations
b. Method of undetermined coefficients
c. Linear differential equation
d. Phase line

17. In trigonometry, the _____ is a function defined as $\tan x = \sin x / \cos x$. The function is so-named because it can be defined as the length of a certain segment of a _____ (in the geometric sense) to the unit circle. In plane geometry, a line is _____ to a curve, at some point, if both line and curve pass through the point with the same direction.
a. Projective connection
b. Hopf conjectures
c. Conformal geometry
d. Tangent

18. In geometry, the _____ to a curve at a given point is the straight line that 'just touches' the curve at that point. As it passes through the point of tangency, the _____ is 'going in the same direction' as the curve, and in this sense it is the best straight-line approximation to the curve at that point. The same definition applies to space curves and curves in n-dimensional Euclidean space.
a. Tangent line
b. Chern-Weil theory
c. Four-vertex theorem
d. Darboux frame

19. In mathematics, a _____ is the end result of a division problem. It can also be expressed as the number of times the divisor divides into the dividend.
a. Notation
b. Limiting
c. Marginal cost
d. Quotient

20. In calculus, the _____ is a formula for the derivative of the composite of two functions.

In intuitive terms, if a variable, y, depends on a second variable, u, which in turn depends on a third variable, x, then the rate of change of y with respect to x can be computed as the rate of change of y with respect to u multiplied by the rate of change of u with respect to x. Schematically,

$$\frac{dy}{dx} = \frac{dy}{du} \cdot \frac{du}{dx}.$$

For an explanation of notation used in this section, see Function composition.

The _____ states that, under appropriate conditions,

$$(f \circ g)'(x) = f'(g(x))g'(x),$$

which in short form is written as

$$(f \circ g)' = f' \circ g \cdot g'.$$

Alternatively, in the Leibniz notation, the _____ is

$$\frac{dy}{dx} = \frac{dy}{du} \cdot \frac{du}{dx}.$$

In integration, the counterpart to the _____ is the substitution rule.

a. 120-cell
c. Product rule

b. 1-center problem
d. Chain rule

21. This article will state and prove the _____ for differentiation, and then use it to prove these two formulas.

The _____ for differentiation states that for every natural number n, the derivative of $f(x) = x^n$ is $f'(x) = nx^{n-1}$, that is,

$$(x^n)' = nx^{n-1}.$$

The _____ for integration

$$\int x^n \, dx = \frac{x^{n+1}}{n+1} + C$$

for natural n is then an easy consequence. One just needs to take the derivative of this equality and use the _____ and linearity of differentiation on the right-hand side.

a. Standard part function
b. Power rule
c. Periodic function
d. Functional integration

22. _____ is to give an equation R(x,y) = S(x,y) that at least in part has the same graph as y = f(x).
a. Implicit function
b. Ordinary differential equation
c. Inflection point
d. Implicit differentiation

23. _____, a field in mathematics, is the study of how functions change when their inputs change. The primary object of study in _____ is the derivative. A closely related notion is the differential.
a. Geometric function theory
b. Semi-continuity
c. Differential calculus
d. Harmonic analysis

24. In mathematics, hyperbolic n-space, denoted H^n, is the maximally symmetric, simply connected, n-dimensional Riemannian manifold with constant sectional curvature −1. _____ is the principal example of a space exhibiting hyperbolic geometry. It can be thought of as the negative-curvature analogue of the n-sphere.
a. Margulis lemma
b. Horocycle
c. Hyperbolic geometry
d. Hyperbolic space

25. Price _____ is defined as the measure of responsivenesses in the quantity demanded for a commodity as a result of change in price of the same commodity.In other words, it is percentage change in quantity demanded as per the percentage change in price of the same commodity. In economics and business studies, the price _____ is a measure of the sensitivity of quantity demanded to changes in price. It is measured as elasticity, that is it measures the relationship as the ratio of percentage changes between quantity demanded of a good and changes in its price.
a. A posteriori
b. A Mathematical Theory of Communication
c. A chemical equation
d. Elasticity of demand

26. In mathematics, a _____ is a statement that can be proved on the basis of explicitly stated or previously agreed assumptions.
a. Logical value
b. Disjunction introduction
c. Boolean function
d. Theorem

27. In mathematics, the interior of a set S consists of all points of S that are intuitively 'not on the edge of S'. A point that is in the interior of S is an _____ of S.

The exterior of a set is the interior of its complement; it consists of the points that are not in the set or its boundary.

a. A posteriori
b. A chemical equation
c. A Mathematical Theory of Communication
d. Interior point

28. In mathematics, a _____ is a way of expressing a number as a fraction of 100. It is often denoted using the percent sign, '%'. For example, 45% is equal to 45 / 100, or 0.45.

a. Least common multiple
b. Percentage
c. Subtrahend
d. Lowest common denominator

Chapter 12. Graphing and Optimization

1. In calculus, a function f defined on a subset of the real numbers with real values is called monotonic (also monotonically increasing or non-_____), if for all x and y such that x ≤ y one has f(x) ≤ f(y), so f preserves the order. In layman's terms, the sign of the slope is always positive (the curve tending upwards) or zero (i.e., non-_____, or asymptotic, or depicted as a horizontal, flat line) Likewise, a function is called monotonically _____ (non-increasing) if, whenever x ≤ y, then f(x) ≥ f(y), so it reverses the order.
    a. Circular convolution
    b. Tensor product of Hilbert spaces
    c. Dual pair
    d. Decreasing

2. The mathematical concept of a _____ expresses the intuitive idea of deterministic dependence between two quantities, one of which is viewed as primary and the other as secondary. A _____ then is a way to associate a unique output for each input of a specified type, for example, a real number or an element of a given set.
    a. Function
    b. Coherent
    c. Going up
    d. Grill

3. In differential topology, a _____ of a differentiable function between differentiable manifolds is the image of a critical point.

    The basic result on _____s is Sard's lemma. The set of _____s can be quite irregular; but in Morse theory it becomes important to consider real-valued functions on a manifold M, such that the set of _____s is in fact finite.

    a. Critical value
    b. Toeplitz operator
    c. Laplacian vector field
    d. Spectral set

4. In number theory, a _____ of a positive integer n is a way of writing n as a sum of positive integers. Two sums which only differ in the order of their summands are considered to be the same _____; if order matters then the sum becomes a composition. A summand in a _____ is also called a part.
    a. Derivative algebra
    b. Congruent
    c. Partition
    d. Distribution

5. A real-valued function f defined on the real line is said to have a _____ point at the point x∗, if there exists some ε > 0, such that f when x − x∗ < ε.
    a. Calculus controversy
    b. Binomial series
    c. Hyperbolic angle
    d. Local maximum

6. In mathematics, _____ and undefined are used to explain whether or not expressions have meaningful, sensible, and unambiguous values. Not all branches of mathematics come to the same conclusion.

    The following expressions are undefined in all contexts, but remarks in the analysis section may apply.

    a. Toy model
    b. Plugging in
    c. LHS
    d. Defined

7. A _____ is a software program that facilitates symbolic mathematics. The core functionality of a CAS is manipulation of mathematical expressions in symbolic form.

Chapter 12. Graphing and Optimization 87

The symbolic manipulations supported typically include

- simplification to the smallest possible expression or some standard form, including automatic simplification with assumptions and simplification with constraints
- substitution of symbolic, functors or numeric values for expressions
- change of form of expressions: expanding products and powers, partial and full factorization, rewriting as partial fractions, constraint satisfaction, rewriting trigonometric functions as exponentials, etc.
- partial and total differentiation
- symbolic constrained and unconstrained global optimization
- solution of linear and some non-linear equations over various domains
- solution of some differential and difference equations
- taking some limits
- some indefinite and definite integration, including multidimensional integrals
- integral transforms
- arbitrary-precision numeric operations
- Series operations such as expansion, summation and products
- matrix operations including products, inverses, etc.
- display of mathematical expressions in two-dimensional mathematical form, often using typesetting systems similar to TeX
- add-ons for use in applied mathematics such as physics packages for physical computation
- plotting graphs and parametric plots of functions in two and three dimensions, and animating them
- APIs for linking it on an external program such as a database, or using in a programming language to use the _____
- drawing charts and diagrams
- string manipulation such as matching and searching
- statistical computation
- Theorem proving and verification
- graphic production and editing such as CGI and signal processing as image processing
- sound synthesis

Many also include a programming language, allowing users to implement their own algorithms.

Some _____s focus on a specific area of application; these are typically developed in academia and are free.

a. 1-center problem
c. 2-3 heap
b. 120-cell
d. Computer algebra system

8. _____s is the social science that studies the production, distribution, and consumption of goods and services.

The term _____s comes from the Ancient Greek oá¼°κονομῐα (oikonomia, 'management of a household, administration') from oá¼¶κος (oikos, 'house') + vÏŒμος (nomos, 'custom' or 'law'), hence 'rules of the house(hold)'.

Current _____ models developed out of the broader field of political economy in the late 19th century, owing to a desire to use an empirical approach more akin to the physical sciences.

a. A chemical equation
b. Experimental economics
c. A Mathematical Theory of Communication
d. Economic

9. In mathematics, a _____ is an expression constructed from variables and constants, using the operations of addition, subtraction, multiplication, and constant non-negative whole number exponents. For example, $x^2 - 4x + 7$ is a _____, but $x^2 - 4/x + 7x^{3/2}$ is not, because its second term involves division by the variable x and also because its third term contains an exponent that is not a whole number.

_____s are one of the most important concepts in algebra and throughout mathematics and science.

a. Semifield
b. Coimage
c. Group extension
d. Polynomial

10. In mathematics, a _____ is any function which can be written as the ratio of two polynomial functions. _____ of degree 2 :

$$y = \frac{x^2 - 3x - 2}{x^2 - 4}$$

In the case of one variable, x, a _____ is a function of the form

$$f(x) = \frac{P(x)}{Q(x)}$$

where P and Q are polynomial function in x and Q is not the zero polynomial. The domain of f is the set of all points x for which the denominator Q

a. 120-cell
b. Rational function
c. Legendre rational functions
d. 1-center problem

11. Let f be a differentiable function, and let f'(x) be its derivative. The derivative of f'(x) (if it has one) is written f''(x) and is called the _____ of f. Similarly, the derivative of a _____, if it exists, is written f'''(x) and is called the third derivative of f.

a. 2-3 heap
b. 1-center problem
c. Second derivative
d. 120-cell

12. The word _____ means curving in or hollowed inward.

a. Clipping
b. Key server
c. Concavity
d. Harmonic series

Chapter 12. Graphing and Optimization

13. _____ is a fundamental construction of differential calculus and admits many possible generalizations within the fields of mathematical analysis, combinatorics, algebra, and geometry.

In real, complex, and functional analysis, _____s are generalized to functions of several real or complex variables and functions between topological vector spaces. An important case is the variational _____ in the calculus of variations.

a. Derivative
b. Functional derivative
c. Lin-Tsien equation
d. Metric derivative

14. In mathematics, _____ and minima, known collectively as extrema, are the largest value or smallest value, that a function takes in a point either within a given neighbourhood or on the function domain in its entirety.

A real-valued function f' defined on the real line is said to have a local maximum point at the point x^*, if there exists some $\varepsilon > 0$, such that f≥ f½x − x^* | < ε. The value of the function at this point is called maximum of the function.

a. Descent
b. Field
c. Decimal system
d. Maxima

15. _____ are points in the domain of a function at which the function takes a largest value or smallest value, either within a given neighborhood or on the function domain in its entirety.

a. Minima
b. Test for Divergence
c. Calculus controversy
d. Maxima and minima

16. In mathematics, maxima and _____, known collectively as extrema, are the largest value or smallest value, that a function takes in a point either within a given neighbourhood or on the function domain in its entirety.

A real-valued function f' defined on the real line is said to have a local maximum point at the point x^*, if there exists some $\varepsilon > 0$, such that f≥ f½x − x^* | < ε. The value of the function at this point is called maximum of the function.

a. Minima
b. Dirichlet integral
c. Calculus
d. Periodic function

17. In differential calculus, an _____, or point of inflection is a point on a curve at which the curvature changes sign. The curve changes from being concave upwards to concave downwards, or vice versa. If one imagines driving a vehicle along the curve, it is a point at which the steering-wheel is momentarily 'straight', being turned from left to right or vice versa.

a. Inflection point
b. Ordinary differential equation
c. Implicit function
d. Implicit differentiation

18. In mathematics, the concept of a _____ tries to capture the intuitive idea of a geometrical one-dimensional and continuous object. A simple example is the circle. In everyday use of the term '_____', a straight line is not curved, but in mathematical parlance _____s include straight lines and line segments.

a. Kappa curve
b. Quadrifolium
c. Negative pedal curve
d. Curve

19. In mathematics, the concept of a '_____' is used to describe the behavior of a function as its argument or input either 'gets close' to some point, or as the argument becomes arbitrarily large; or the behavior of a sequence's elements as their index increases indefinitely. _____s are used in calculus and other branches of mathematical analysis to define derivatives and continuity.

In formulas, _____ is usually abbreviated as lim.

a. Limit
b. Copula
c. Duality
d. Contact

20. In mathematics, more precisely in algebra, an _____ is a quantity that is not known, and cannot be solved for. An _____ is different from a variable, which is solvable, at least conditionally, from a given equation or set of equations. To make this distinction in an example, compare these two situations.

a. Algebraic function
b. Indeterminate
c. Immanant of a matrix
d. Algebraic solution

21. In calculus and other branches of mathematical analysis, an _____ is an algebraic expression obtained in the context of limits. Limits involving algebraic operations are often performed by replacing subexpressions by their limits; if the expression obtained after this substitution does not give enough information to determine the original limit, it is known as an _____. The _____s include 0^0, $0/0$, 1^∞, $\infty - \infty$, ∞/∞, $0 \times \infty$, and ∞^0.

a. Improper integral
b. Exponential function can be characterized
c. Uniformly absolutely continuous
d. Indeterminate form

22. In mathematics, a _____ of a set S in a topological space X is a point x in X that can be 'approximated' by points of S other than x itself. This concept profitably generalizes the notion of a limit and is the underpinning of concepts such as closed set and topological closure. Indeed, a set is closed if and only if it contains all of its _____s, and the topological closure operation can be thought of as an operation that enriches a set by adding its _____s.

a. 1-center problem
b. 120-cell
c. Limit point
d. 2-3 heap

23. Any formula written in terms of logarithms may be said to be in _____.

In contexts including complex manifolds and algebraic geometry, a logarithmic differential form is a 1-form that, locally at least, can be written

$$\frac{df}{f}$$

for some meromorphic function f. That is, for some open covering, there are local representations of this differential form as a logarithmic derivative.

Chapter 12. Graphing and Optimization

a. Laurent series
b. Holomorphic sheaf
c. Cauchy-Hadamard theorem
d. Logarithmic form

24. In mathematics, hyperbolic n-space, denoted H^n, is the maximally symmetric, simply connected, n-dimensional Riemannian manifold with constant sectional curvature −1. _____ is the principal example of a space exhibiting hyperbolic geometry. It can be thought of as the negative-curvature analogue of the n-sphere.
   a. Horocycle
   b. Hyperbolic geometry
   c. Hyperbolic space
   d. Margulis lemma

25. In mathematics, a _____ is a statement that can be proved on the basis of explicitly stated or previously agreed assumptions.
   a. Disjunction introduction
   b. Theorem
   c. Boolean function
   d. Logical value

26. In calculus, a _____ is either of the two limits of a function f

$$\lim_{x \to a^+} f(x) \text{ or } \lim_{x \downarrow a} f(x)$$

for the limit as x approaches a from above, and similarly

$$\lim_{x \to a^-} f(x) \text{ or } \lim_{x \uparrow a} f(x)$$

for the limit as x approaches a from below.

The two _____s exist and are equal if and only if the limit of f

   a. Archimedes' use of infinitesimals
   b. Infinite series
   c. One-sided limit
   d. Uniform convergence

27. _____ is the state of being greater than any finite number, however large.
   a. A Mathematical Theory of Communication
   b. Implicit differentiation
   c. Interval notation
   d. Infinity

28. An _____ of a real-valued function y = f(x) is a curve which describes the behavior of f as either x or y tends to infinity.

In other words, as one moves along the graph of f(x) in some direction, the distance between it and the _____ eventually becomes smaller than any distance that one may specify.

If a curve A has the curve B as an _____, one says that A is asymptotic to B. Similarly B is asymptotic to A, so A and B are called asymptotic.

a. Infinite product
c. Isoperimetric dimension
b. Asymptote
d. Improper integral

29. In game theory, a player's _____ in a game is a complete plan of action for whatever situation might arise; this fully determines the player's behaviour. A player's _____ will determine the action the player will take at any stage of the game, for every possible history of play up to that stage.

A _____ profile is a set of strategies for each player which fully specifies all actions in a game.

a. Matching pennies
c. Sir Philip Sidney game
b. Correlated equilibrium
d. Strategy

30. In mathematics, an _____, or central tendency of a data set refers to a measure of the 'middle' or 'expected' value of the data set. There are many different descriptive statistics that can be chosen as a measurement of the central tendency of the data items.

An _____ is a single value that is meant to typify a list of values.

a. A Mathematical Theory of Communication
c. A chemical equation
b. A posteriori
d. Average

31. In economics, _____ is equal to total cost divided by the number of goods produced Quantity-Q. It is also equal to the sum of average variable costs total variable costs divided by Q plus average fixed costs total fixed costs divided by Q. _____s may be dependent on the time period considered increasing production may be expensive or impossible in the short term, for example. _____s affect the supply curve and are a fundamental component of supply and demand.

a. Extreme value theorem
c. Equity
b. Uncertainty quantification
d. Average cost

32. In economics, business, retail, and accounting, a _____ is the value of money that has been used up to produce something, and hence is not available for use anymore. In business, the _____ may be one of acquisition, in which case the amount of money expended to acquire it is counted as _____. In this case, money is the input that is gone in order to acquire the thing.

a. 120-cell
c. Cost
b. 1-center problem
d. 2-3 heap

33. In calculus, the _____ states that if a real-valued function f is continuous in the closed interval, then f must attain its maximum and minimum value, each at least once.

a. Equity
c. Uncertainty quantification
b. Average cost
d. Extreme value theorem

34. In mathematics, a _____ is a set of real numbers with the property that any number that lies between two numbers in the set is also included in the set. For example, the set of all numbers x satisfying $0 \leq x \leq 1$ is an _____ which contains 0 and 1, as well as all numbers between them. Other examples of _____s are the set of all real numbers $\mathbb{R}$, the set of all positive real numbers, and the empty set.

a. Order
c. Ideal
b. Annihilator
d. Interval

35. In calculus, a branch of mathematics, the _____ determines whether a given stationary point of a function is a maximum or a minimum.
   a. Barrelled spaces
   c. Second-derivative test
   b. Christofides heuristics algorithm
   d. Cook reduction

36. _____ methods are common techniques to compute the equilibrium configuration of molecules. The basic idea is that a stable state of a molecular system should correspond to a local minimum of their potential energy. This kind of calculation generally starts from an arbitrary state of molecules, then the mathematical procedure of optimization allows us to move atoms in a way to reduce the net forces to nearly zero.
   a. A Mathematical Theory of Communication
   c. A posteriori
   b. Energy minimization
   d. A chemical equation

37. In mathematics and computer science, an _____ is the problem of finding the best solution from all feasible solutions. More formally, an _____ A is a quadruple , where

   - I is a set of instances;
   - given an instance $x \in I$, f is the set of feasible solutions;
   - given an instance x and a feasible solution y of x, m denotes the measure of y, which is usually a positive real.
   - g is the goal function, and is either min or max.

The goal is then to find for some instance x an optimal solution, that is, a feasible solution y with

$$m(x, y) = g\{m(x, y') \mid y' \in f(x)\}.$$

For each _____, there is a corresponding decision problem that asks whether there is a feasible solution for some particular measure m_0. For example, if there is a graph G which contains vertices u and v, an _____ might be 'find a path from u to v that uses the fewest edges'. This problem might have an answer of, say, 4.

   a. Interactive proof system
   c. Element uniqueness
   b. Optimization problem
   d. Approximation algorithms

38. _____ is a quantity expressing the two-dimensional size of a defined part of a surface, typically a region bounded by a closed curve. The term surface _____ refers to the total _____ of the exposed surface of a 3-dimensional solid, such as the sum of the _____ s of the exposed sides of a polyhedron. _____ is an important invariant in the differential geometry of surfaces.
   a. A chemical equation
   c. A Mathematical Theory of Communication
   b. A posteriori
   d. Area

39. The _____ is the length of the line that bounds an area In the special case where the area is circular, the _____ is known as the circumference.

a. Perimeter
b. Concyclic
c. Reflection symmetry
d. Multilateration

40. The _____ is a type of problem encountered within the field of optimal control. One issue is infrequent large orders vs. frequent small orders.

a. Elementary proof
b. Iverson bracket
c. Inventory control problem
d. Exponential error

Chapter 13. Integration

1. In grammatical theory, definiteness is a feature of noun phrases, distinguishing between entities which are specific and identifiable in a given context (_____ noun phrases) and entities which are not (indefinite noun phrases Examples are:

- Free form: English the boy.
- Phrasal clitic: as in Basque: Cf. emakume ('woman'), emakume-a (woman-ART: 'the woman'), emakume ederr-a (woman beautiful-ART: 'the beautiful woman')
- Noun affix: as in Romanian: om ('man'), om-ul (man-ART: 'the man'); om-ul bun (man-ART good: 'the good man')
- Prefix on both noun and adjective: Arabic Ø§Ù„ÙƒØªØ§Ø¨ Ø§Ù„ÙƒØ¨ÙŠØ± (al-kitÄ b al-kabÄ«r) with two instances of al- (DEF-book-DEF-big, literally, 'the book the big')

Germanic, Romance, Celtic, Semitic, and auxiliary languages generally have a _____ article, sometimes used as a postposition. Many other languages do not.

a. Sentence diagram
b. 1-center problem
c. Syntax
d. Definite

2. The _____ specifies the relationship between the two central operations of calculus, differentiation and integration.

The first part of the theorem, sometimes called the first _____, shows that an indefinite integration can be reversed by a differentiation.

The second part, sometimes called the second _____, allows one to compute the definite integral of a function by using any one of its infinitely many antiderivatives.

a. Standard part function
b. Fundamental theorem of calculus
c. Hyperbolic angle
d. Maxima and minima

3. In calculus, an antiderivative, primitive or _____ of a function f is a function F whose derivative is equal to f. The process of solving for antiderivatives is antidifferentiation. Antiderivatives are related to definite integrals through the fundamental theorem of calculus, and provide a convenient means for calculating the definite integrals of many functions.

a. Integration by parts operator
b. Indefinite integral
c. Integral
d. Integral test for convergence

4. In commutative algebra, the notions of an element _____ over a ring, and of an _____ extension of rings, are a generalization of the notions in field theory of an element being algebraic over a field, and of an algebraic extension of fields.

The special case of greatest interest in number theory is that of complex numbers _____ over the ring of integers Z.

The term ring will be understood to mean commutative ring with a unit.

a. Arc length
b. Integral test for convergence
c. Antidifferentiation
d. Integral

5. _____ is a core concept of basic mathematics, specifically in the fields of infinitesimal calculus and mathematical analysis. Given a function f

$$\int_a^b f(x)\,dx,$$

is equal to the area of a region in the xy-plane bounded by the graph of f, the x-axis, and the vertical lines x = a and x = b, with areas below the x-axis being subtracted.

The term 'integral' may also refer to the notion of antiderivative, a function F whose derivative is the given function f.

a. OMAC
b. Integration
c. Apex
d. Epigraph

6. _____ is a branch of mathematics that includes the study of limits, derivatives, integrals, and infinite series, and constitutes a major part of modern university education. Historically, it has been referred to as 'the _____ of infinitesimals', or 'infinitesimal _____'. Most basically, _____ is the study of change, in the same way that geometry is the study of space.

a. Calculus
b. Test for Divergence
c. Partial sum
d. Hyperbolic angle

7. In mathematics, a _____ is a statement that can be proved on the basis of explicitly stated or previously agreed assumptions.

a. Boolean function
b. Logical value
c. Disjunction introduction
d. Theorem

8. In complex analysis, a branch of mathematics, the _____ of a complex-valued function g is a function whose complex derivative is g. More precisely, given an open set U in the complex plane and a function $g : U \to \mathbb{C}$, the _____ of g is a function $f : U \to \mathbb{C}$ that satisfies $\frac{df}{dz} = g$.

As such, this concept is the complex-variable version of the _____ of a real-valued function.

a. Integration by parts
b. Indefinite integral
c. Integral
d. Antiderivative

9. In mathematics and in the sciences, a _____ (plural: _____e, formulæ or _____s) is a concise way of expressing information symbolically (as in a mathematical or chemical _____), or a general relationship between quantities. One of many famous _____e is Albert Einstein's E = mc² (see special relativity)

In mathematics, a _____ is a key to solve an equation with variables. For example, the problem of determining the volume of a sphere is one that requires a significant amount of integral calculus to solve.

a. Formula
b. 2-3 heap
c. 1-center problem
d. 120-cell

10. In mathematics, _____ and undefined are used to explain whether or not expressions have meaningful, sensible, and unambiguous values. Not all branches of mathematics come to the same conclusion.

The following expressions are undefined in all contexts, but remarks in the analysis section may apply.

a. Plugging in
c. Toy model

b. LHS
d. Defined

11. The mathematical concept of a _____ expresses the intuitive idea of deterministic dependence between two quantities, one of which is viewed as primary and the other as secondary. A _____ then is a way to associate a unique output for each input of a specified type, for example, a real number or an element of a given set.

a. Going up
c. Grill

b. Coherent
d. Function

12. A _____ is a software program that facilitates symbolic mathematics. The core functionality of a CAS is manipulation of mathematical expressions in symbolic form.

The symbolic manipulations supported typically include

- simplification to the smallest possible expression or some standard form, including automatic simplification with assumptions and simplification with constraints
- substitution of symbolic, functors or numeric values for expressions
- change of form of expressions: expanding products and powers, partial and full factorization, rewriting as partial fractions, constraint satisfaction, rewriting trigonometric functions as exponentials, etc.
- partial and total differentiation
- symbolic constrained and unconstrained global optimization
- solution of linear and some non-linear equations over various domains
- solution of some differential and difference equations
- taking some limits
- some indefinite and definite integration, including multidimensional integrals
- integral transforms
- arbitrary-precision numeric operations
- Series operations such as expansion, summation and products
- matrix operations including products, inverses, etc.
- display of mathematical expressions in two-dimensional mathematical form, often using typesetting systems similar to TeX
- add-ons for use in applied mathematics such as physics packages for physical computation
- plotting graphs and parametric plots of functions in two and three dimensions, and animating them
- APIs for linking it on an external program such as a database, or using in a programming language to use the _____
- drawing charts and diagrams
- string manipulation such as matching and searching
- statistical computation
- Theorem proving and verification
- graphic production and editing such as CGI and signal processing as image processing
- sound synthesis

Many also include a programming language, allowing users to implement their own algorithms.

Some _____s focus on a specific area of application; these are typically developed in academia and are free.

a. Computer algebra system
b. 2-3 heap
c. 1-center problem
d. 120-cell

13. In mathematics, the concept of a _____ tries to capture the intuitive idea of a geometrical one-dimensional and continuous object. A simple example is the circle. In everyday use of the term '_____', a straight line is not curved, but in mathematical parlance _____s include straight lines and line segments.
a. Kappa curve
b. Quadrifolium
c. Negative pedal curve
d. Curve

Chapter 13. Integration

14. In economics, business, retail, and accounting, a _____ is the value of money that has been used up to produce something, and hence is not available for use anymore. In business, the _____ may be one of acquisition, in which case the amount of money expended to acquire it is counted as _____. In this case, money is the input that is gone in order to acquire the thing.
   a. Cost
   b. 2-3 heap
   c. 1-center problem
   d. 120-cell

15. In economics, the cross elasticity of demand and _____ measures the responsiveness of the quantity demanded of a good to a change in the price of another good.

It is measured as the percentage change in quantity demanded for the first good that occurs in response to a percentage change in price of the second good. For example, if, in response to a 10% increase in the price of fuel, the quantity of new cars that are fuel inefficient demanded decreased by 20%, the cross elasticity of demand would be -20%/10% = -2.

   a. Cross price elasticity of demand
   b. 1-center problem
   c. Marginal rate of substitution
   d. Supply and demand

16. In calculus, _____ is a tool for finding antiderivatives and integrals. Using the fundamental theorem of calculus often requires finding an antiderivative. For this and other reasons, _____ is a relatively important tool for mathematicians.
   a. Integration by substitution
   b. One-sided limit
   c. Uniform convergence
   d. Interpolation

17. In calculus, the _____ is a formula for the derivative of the composite of two functions.

In intuitive terms, if a variable, y, depends on a second variable, u, which in turn depends on a third variable, x, then the rate of change of y with respect to x can be computed as the rate of change of y with respect to u multiplied by the rate of change of u with respect to x. Schematically,

$$\frac{dy}{dx} = \frac{dy}{du} \cdot \frac{du}{dx}.$$

For an explanation of notation used in this section, see Function composition.

The _____ states that, under appropriate conditions,

$$(f \circ g)'(x) = f'(g(x))g'(x),$$

which in short form is written as

$$(f \circ g)' = f' \circ g \cdot g'.$$

Alternatively, in the Leibniz notation, the _____ is

$$\frac{dy}{dx} = \frac{dy}{du} \cdot \frac{du}{dx}.$$

In integration, the counterpart to the _____ is the substitution rule.

a. Product rule
c. 120-cell

b. 1-center problem
d. Chain rule

18. Suppose that φ : M → N is a smooth map between smooth manifolds; then the _____ of φ at a point x is, in some sense, the best linear approximation of φ near x. It can be viewed as generalization of the total derivative of ordinary calculus. Explicitly, it is a linear map from the tangent space of M at x to the tangent space of N at φ

a. Grill
c. Boundary

b. Concurrent
d. Differential

19. _____s is concerned with the tasks of developing and applying quantitative or statistical methods to the study and elucidation of economic principles. _____s combines economic theory with statistics to analyze and test economic relationships. Theoretical _____s considers questions about the statistical properties of estimators and tests, while applied _____s is concerned with the application of _____ methods to assess economic theories.

a. A chemical equation
c. Economic

b. Econometric
d. A Mathematical Theory of Communication

20. _____s arise in many problems in physics, engineering, etc. The following examples show how to solve _____s in a few simple cases when an exact solution exists.

A separable linear ordinary _____ of the first order has the general form:

$$\frac{dy}{dt} + f(t)y = 0$$

where f is some known function.

a. Nullcline
c. Nahm equations

b. Homogeneous differential equation
d. Differential equation

21. In mathematics, an _____ is a relation that contains functions of only one independent variable, and one or more of its derivatives with respect to that variable.

A simple example is Newton's second law of motion, which leads to the differential equation

$$m\frac{d^2x(t)}{dt^2} = F(x(t)),$$

for the motion of a particle of mass m. In general, the force F depends upon the position of the particle at time t, and thus the unknown function appears on both sides of the differential equation, as is indicated in the notation F

a. Implicit differentiation
c. Inflection point
b. Implicit function
d. Ordinary differential equation

22. _____ is a phenomenon which arises in the region of a continuous phase transition. Originally reported by Thomas Andrews in 1869 for the liquid-gas transition in carbon dioxide, many other examples have been discovered since. The phenomenon is most commonly demonstrated in binary fluid mixtures, such as methanol and cyclohexane.
a. Critical opalescence
c. Fermi point
b. Percolation threshold
d. Critical temperature

23. _____ is used to describe the steepness, incline, gradient, or grade of a straight line. A higher _____ value indicates a steeper incline. The _____ is defined as the ratio of the 'rise' divided by the 'run' between two points on a line, or in other words, the ratio of the altitude change to the horizontal distance between any two points on the line.
a. Slope
c. Point plotting
b. Cognitively Guided Instruction
d. Number line

24. In abstract algebra, a _____ is an algebraic structure in which the operations of addition, subtraction, multiplication and division may be performed in a way that satisfies some familiar rules from the arithmetic of ordinary numbers.

All _____s are rings, but not conversely. _____s differ from rings most importantly in the requirement that division be possible, but also, in modern definitions, by the requirement that the multiplication operation in a _____ be commutative.

a. Chord
c. Blind
b. Functional
d. Field

25. In probability theory, a probability distribution is called _____ if its cumulative distribution function is _____. That is equivalent to saying that for random variables X with the distribution in question, Pr[X = a] = 0 for all real numbers a. If the distribution of X is _____ then X is called a _____ random variable.
a. Conull set
c. Continuous
b. Continuous phase modulation
d. Concatenated codes

26. _____ is the concept of adding accumulated interest back to the principal, so that interest is earned on interest from that moment on. The act of declaring interest to be principal is called compounding. A loan, for example, may have its interest compounded every month: in this case, a loan with $100 principal and 1% interest per month would have a balance of $101 at the end of the first month.
a. Retained interest
c. Compound interest
b. Net interest margin
d. Net interest margin securities

27. _____ is a fee, paid on borrowed capital. Assets lent include money, shares, consumer goods through hire purchase, major assets such as aircraft, and even entire factories in finance lease arrangements. The _____ is calculated upon the value of the assets in the same manner as upon money.

a. A Mathematical Theory of Communication
b. Interest sensitivity gap
c. Interest expense
d. Interest

28. A quantity is said to be subject to _____ if it decreases at a rate proportional to its value. Symbolically, this can be expressed as the following differential equation, where N is the quantity and λ is a positive number called the decay constant.

$$\frac{dN}{dt} = -\lambda N.$$

The solution to this equation is:

$$N(t) = N_0 e^{-\lambda t}.$$

Here is the quantity at time t, and N_0 = N is the quantity, at time t = 0.

a. Exponentiating by squaring
b. Exponential integral
c. Exponential formula
d. Exponential decay

29. _____ occurs when the growth rate of a mathematical function is proportional to the function's current value. In the case of a discrete domain of definition with equal intervals it is also called geometric growth or geometric decay.

With _____ of a positive value its rate of increase steadily increases, or in the case of exponential decay, its rate of decrease steadily decreases.

a. Exponential growth
b. A chemical equation
c. A Mathematical Theory of Communication
d. A posteriori

30. _____ is the change in population over time, and can be quantified as the change in the number of individuals in a population using 'per unit time' for measurement. The term _____ can technically refer to any species, but almost always refers to humans, and it is often used informally for the more specific demographic term _____ rate, and is often used to refer specifically to the growth of the population of the world.

Simple models of _____ include the Malthusian Growth Model and the logistic model.

a. 1-center problem
b. Population growth
c. 120-cell
d. Population dynamics

31. _____ is the process in which an unstable atomic nucleus loses energy by emitting ionizing particles and radiation. This decay, or loss of energy, results in an atom of one type, called the parent nuclide transforming to an atom of a different type, called the daughter nuclide. For example: a carbon-14 atom emits radiation and transforms to a nitrogen-14 atom.
a. 120-cell
b. 1-center problem
c. Half-life
d. Radioactive decay

Chapter 13. Integration

32. _____ is a quantity expressing the two-dimensional size of a defined part of a surface, typically a region bounded by a closed curve. The term surface _____ refers to the total _____ of the exposed surface of a 3-dimensional solid, such as the sum of the _____s of the exposed sides of a polyhedron. _____ is an important invariant in the differential geometry of surfaces.
   a. A chemical equation
   c. A Mathematical Theory of Communication
   b. A posteriori
   d. Area

33. The most common _____ are left, right, forward, backward, up, and down. No absolute direction corresponds to any of the _____. This is a consequence of the translational invariance of the laws of physics: nature, loosely speaking, behaves the same no matter what direction one moves.
   a. Christofides heuristics
   c. CM-type
   b. Relative directions
   d. Convex and concave

34. In mathematics, the concept of a '_____' is used to describe the behavior of a function as its argument or input either 'gets close' to some point, or as the argument becomes arbitrarily large; or the behavior of a sequence's elements as their index increases indefinitely. _____s are used in calculus and other branches of mathematical analysis to define derivatives and continuity.

In formulas, _____ is usually abbreviated as lim.

   a. Duality
   c. Contact
   b. Copula
   d. Limit

35. In mathematics, a _____ of a set S in a topological space X is a point x in X that can be 'approximated' by points of S other than x itself. This concept profitably generalizes the notion of a limit and is the underpinning of concepts such as closed set and topological closure. Indeed, a set is closed if and only if it contains all of its _____s, and the topological closure operation can be thought of as an operation that enriches a set by adding its _____s.
   a. 2-3 heap
   c. 1-center problem
   b. Limit point
   d. 120-cell

36. Georg Friedrich Bernhard _____ was a German mathematician who made important contributions to analysis and differential geometry, some of them paving the way for the later development of general relativity.

_____ was born in Breselenz, a village near Dannenberg in the Kingdom of Hanover in what is today Germany. His father, Friedrich Bernhard _____, was a poor Lutheran pastor in Breselenz who fought in the Napoleonic Wars.

   a. Brook Taylor
   c. Riemann
   b. Paul C. van Oorschot
   d. Gustave Bertrand

37. In mathematics, a _____ is a method for approximating the total area underneath a curve on a graph, otherwise known as an integral. It may also be used to define the integration operation. The sums are named after the German mathematician Bernhard Riemann.
   a. Singular measure
   c. Multiple integral
   b. Solid of revolution
   d. Riemann sum

Chapter 13. Integration

38. _____ is the addition of a set of numbers; the result is their sum or total. An interim or present total of a _____ process is termed the running total. The 'numbers' to be summed may be natural numbers, complex numbers, matrices, or still more complicated objects.
- a. 1-center problem
- b. 120-cell
- c. 2-3 heap
- d. Summation

39. _____ is the change in total cost that arises when the quantity produced changes by one unit.
- a. Marginal cost
- b. Notation
- c. Limiting
- d. Differential Algebra

40. A _____ typically refers to a class of handheld calculators that are capable of plotting graphs, solving simultaneous equations, and performing numerous other tasks with variables. Most popular _____s are also programmable, allowing the user to create customized programs, typically for scientific/engineering and education applications. Due to their large displays intended for graphing, they can also accommodate several lines of text and calculations at a time.
- a. Graphing calculator
- b. Bump mapping
- c. Support vector machines
- d. Genus

41. A _____ is a device for performing mathematical calculations, distinguished from a computer by having a limited problem solving ability and an interface optimized for interactive calculation rather than programming. _____s can be hardware or software, and mechanical or electronic, and are often built into devices such as PDAs or mobile phones.

Modern electronic _____s are generally small, digital, and usually inexpensive.

- a. 120-cell
- b. 1-center problem
- c. 2-3 heap
- d. Calculator

42. In mathematics, an _____, or central tendency of a data set refers to a measure of the 'middle' or 'expected' value of the data set. There are many different descriptive statistics that can be chosen as a measurement of the central tendency of the data items.

An _____ is a single value that is meant to typify a list of values.

- a. A posteriori
- b. A Mathematical Theory of Communication
- c. A chemical equation
- d. Average

1. _____ is a quantity expressing the two-dimensional size of a defined part of a surface, typically a region bounded by a closed curve. The term surface _____ refers to the total _____ of the exposed surface of a 3-dimensional solid, such as the sum of the _____s of the exposed sides of a polyhedron. _____ is an important invariant in the differential geometry of surfaces.
   a. A chemical equation
   b. A posteriori
   c. A Mathematical Theory of Communication
   d. Area

2. _____ is a core concept of basic mathematics, specifically in the fields of infinitesimal calculus and mathematical analysis. Given a function f

$$\int_a^b f(x)\, dx,$$

is equal to the area of a region in the xy-plane bounded by the graph of f, the x-axis, and the vertical lines x = a and x = b, with areas below the x-axis being subtracted.

The term 'integral' may also refer to the notion of antiderivative, a function F whose derivative is the given function f.

   a. Apex
   b. Integration
   c. OMAC
   d. Epigraph

3. In mathematics, the concept of a _____ tries to capture the intuitive idea of a geometrical one-dimensional and continuous object. A simple example is the circle. In everyday use of the term '_____', a straight line is not curved, but in mathematical parlance _____s include straight lines and line segments.
   a. Quadrifolium
   b. Curve
   c. Kappa curve
   d. Negative pedal curve

4. The _____ is a graphical representation of the cumulative distribution function of a probability distribution; it is a graph showing the proportion of the distribution assumed by the bottom y% of the values. It is often used to represent income distribution, where it shows for the bottom x% of households, what percentage y% of the total income they have. The percentage of households is plotted on the x-axis, the percentage of income on the y-axis.
   a. Phillips curve
   b. 1-center problem
   c. Demand curve
   d. Lorenz curve

5. The _____ fallacy is an informal fallacy. It ascribes cause where none exists. The flaw is failing to account for natural fluctuations.
   a. Degrees of freedom
   b. Depth
   c. Differential
   d. Regression

6. In statistics, _____ is a collective name for techniques for the modeling and analysis of numerical data consisting of values of a dependent variable and of one or more independent variables. The dependent variable in the regression equation is modeled as a function of the independent variables, corresponding parameters, and an error term. The error term is treated as a random variable.

a. 1-center problem
c. 120-cell
b. 2-3 heap
d. Regression analysis

7. In differential geometry, a discipline within mathematics, a _____ is a subset of the tangent bundle of a manifold satisfying certain properties. _____s are used to build up notions of integrability, and specifically of a foliation of a manifold
   a. Coherence
   b. Distribution
   c. Constraint
   d. Discontinuity

8. In chemistry, _____ is the measure of how much of a given substance there is mixed with another substance. This can apply to any sort of chemical mixture, but most frequently the concept is limited to homogeneous solutions, where it refers to the amount of solute in the solvent.

To concentrate a solution, one must add more solute, or reduce the amount of solvent (for instance, by selective evaporation.)

   a. 1-center problem
   b. 2-3 heap
   c. Concentration
   d. 120-cell

9. In mathematics, an _____ is a statement about the relative size or order of two objects, or about whether they are the same or not

- The notation a < b means that a is less than b.
- The notation a > b means that a is greater than b.
- The notation a ≠ b means that a is not equal to b, but does not say that one is bigger than the other or even that they can be compared in size.

In all these cases, a is not equal to b, hence, '_____'.

These relations are known as strict _____

- The notation a ≤ b means that a is less than or equal to b;
- The notation a ≥ b means that a is greater than or equal to b;

An additional use of the notation is to show that one quantity is much greater than another, normally by several orders of magnitude.

- The notation a << b means that a is much less than b.
- The notation a >> b means that a is much greater than b.

If the sense of the _____ is the same for all values of the variables for which its members are defined, then the _____ is called an 'absolute' or 'unconditional' _____. If the sense of an _____ holds only for certain values of the variables involved, but is reversed or destroyed for other values of the variables, it is called a conditional _____.

Chapter 14. Additional Integration Topics

An _____ may appear unsolvable because it only states whether a number is larger or smaller than another number; but it is possible to apply the same operations for equalities to inequalities. For example, to find x for the _____ 10x > 23 one would divide 23 by 10.

a. A Mathematical Theory of Communication
b. A chemical equation
c. A posteriori
d. Inequality

10. In probability theory, a probability distribution is called _____ if its cumulative distribution function is _____. That is equivalent to saying that for random variables X with the distribution in question, Pr[X = a] = 0 for all real numbers a. If the distribution of X is _____ then X is called a _____ random variable.

a. Conull set
b. Concatenated codes
c. Continuous phase modulation
d. Continuous

11. _____ is the likelihood or chance that something is the case or will happen. Theoretical _____ is used extensively in areas such as statistics, mathematics, science and philosophy to draw conclusions about the likelihood of potential events and the underlying mechanics of complex systems.

The word _____ does not have a consistent direct definition.

a. Statistical significance
b. Standardized moment
c. Discrete random variable
d. Probability

12. In mathematics, a _____ is a function that represents a probability distribution in terms of integrals.

Formally, a probability distribution has density f, if f is a non-negative Lebesgue-integrable function $\mathbb{R} \to \mathbb{R}$ such that the probability of the interval [a, b] is given by

$$\int_a^b f(x)\,dx$$

for any two numbers a and b. This implies that the total integral of f must be 1.

a. Quantile
b. Law of total variance
c. Pseudocount
d. Probability density function

13. In mathematics, _____ and undefined are used to explain whether or not expressions have meaningful, sensible, and unambiguous values. Not all branches of mathematics come to the same conclusion.

The following expressions are undefined in all contexts, but remarks in the analysis section may apply.

a. Plugging in
b. Toy model
c. Defined
d. LHS

14. The _____ of a material is defined as its mass per unit volume:

$$\rho = \frac{m}{V}$$

Different materials usually have different densities, so _____ is an important concept regarding buoyancy, metal purity and packaging.

In some cases _____ is expressed as the dimensionless quantities specific gravity or relative _____, in which case it is expressed in multiples of the _____ of some other standard material, usually water or air.

In a well-known story, Archimedes was given the task of determining whether King Hiero's goldsmith was embezzling gold during the manufacture of a wreath dedicated to the gods and replacing it with another, cheaper alloy.

a. 120-cell
b. 1-center problem
c. Density
d. 2-3 heap

15. The mathematical concept of a _____ expresses the intuitive idea of deterministic dependence between two quantities, one of which is viewed as primary and the other as secondary. A _____ then is a way to associate a unique output for each input of a specified type, for example, a real number or an element of a given set.
a. Going up
b. Coherent
c. Grill
d. Function

16. In mathematics, _____ are used in the study of chance and probability. They were developed to assist in the analysis of games of chance, stochastic events, and the results of scientific experiments by capturing only the mathematical properties necessary to answer probabilistic questions. Further formalizations have firmly grounded the entity in the theoretical domains of mathematics by making use of measure theory.
a. Median polish
b. Random variables
c. Statistical dispersion
d. Statistics

17. In probability theory, a probability distribution is called discrete if it is characterized by a probability mass function. Thus, the distribution of a random variable X is discrete, and X is then called a _____, if

$$\sum_u \Pr(X = u) = 1$$

as u runs through the set of all possible values of X.

If a random variable is discrete, then the set of all values that it can assume with non-zero probability is finite or countably infinite, because the sum of uncountably many positive real numbers always diverges to infinity.

a. Discrete random variable
b. Regression toward the mean
c. First-hitting-time models
d. Statistics

Chapter 14. Additional Integration Topics

18. In mathematics, specifically in combinatorial commutative algebra, a convex lattice polytope P is called _____ if it has the following property: given any positive integer n, every lattice point of the dilation nP, obtained from P by scaling its vertices by the factor n and taking the convex hull of the resulting points, can be written as the sum of exactly n lattice points in P. This property plays an important role in the theory of toric varieties, where it corresponds to projective normality of the toric variety determined by P.

The simplex in R^k with the vertices at the origin and along the unit coordinate vectors is _____.

a. Hypercube
b. Normal
c. Demihypercubes
d. Polytetrahedron

19. In calculus, and more generally in mathematical analysis, _____ is a rule that transforms the integral of products of functions into other, hopefully simpler, integrals. The rule arises from the product rule of differentiation.

If u = f[x], v = g[x], and the differentials du = f '[x] dx and dv = g'[x] dx; then in its simplest form the product rule is:

a. Integration by parts operator
b. Integral test for convergence
c. Arc length
d. Integration by parts

20. In mathematics, hyperbolic n-space, denoted H^n, is the maximally symmetric, simply connected, n-dimensional Riemannian manifold with constant sectional curvature −1. _____ is the principal example of a space exhibiting hyperbolic geometry. It can be thought of as the negative-curvature analogue of the n-sphere.

a. Margulis lemma
b. Hyperbolic space
c. Hyperbolic geometry
d. Horocycle

21. In mathematics and in the sciences, a _____ (plural: _____e, formulæ or _____s) is a concise way of expressing information symbolically (as in a mathematical or chemical _____), or a general relationship between quantities. One of many famous _____e is Albert Einstein's $E = mc^2$ (see special relativity

In mathematics, a _____ is a key to solve an equation with variables. For example, the problem of determining the volume of a sphere is one that requires a significant amount of integral calculus to solve.

a. 1-center problem
b. 120-cell
c. 2-3 heap
d. Formula

22. In commutative algebra, the notions of an element _____ over a ring, and of an _____ extension of rings, are a generalization of the notions in field theory of an element being algebraic over a field, and of an algebraic extension of fields.

The special case of greatest interest in number theory is that of complex numbers _____ over the ring of integers Z.

The term ring will be understood to mean commutative ring with a unit.

a. Integral test for convergence
b. Arc length
c. Antidifferentiation
d. Integral

23. In vascular plants, the _____ is the organ of a plant body that typically lies below the surface of the soil. This is not always the case, however, since a _____ can also be aerial (that is, growing above the ground) or aerating (that is, growing up above the ground or especially above water.) Furthermore, a stem normally occurring below ground is not exceptional either

a. 120-cell
b. 1-center problem
c. Root
d. 2-3 heap

24. In mathematics, a _____ of a number x is a number r such that r^2 = x, or, in other words, a number r whose square is x. Every non-negative real number x has a unique non-negative _____, called the principal _____, which is denoted with a radical symbol as $\sqrt{x}$, or, using exponent notation, as $x^{1/2}$. For example, the principal _____ of 9 is 3, denoted $\sqrt{9}$ = 3, because 3^2 = 3 × 3 = 9.

a. Square root
b. Double exponential
c. Hyperbolic functions
d. Multiplicative inverse

Chapter 15. Multivariable Calculus

1. _____ calculus is the extension of calculus in one variable to calculus in several variables: the functions which are differentiated and integrated involve several variables rather than one variable.
   a. Cook reduction
   b. Convex and concave
   c. Convergence of measures
   d. Multivariable

2. _____ is the extension of calculus in one variable to calculus in several variables: the functions which are differentiated and integrated involve several variables rather than one variable.

A study of limits and continuity in multiple dimensions yields many counter-intuitive and pathological results not demonstrated by single-variable functions. There exist, for example, scalar functions of two variables having points in their domain which, when approached along any arbitrary line, give a particular limit, yet give a different limit when approached along a parabola.

   a. Multivariable calculus
   b. Shift theorem
   c. Surface integral
   d. Total derivative

3. _____ is a branch of mathematics that includes the study of limits, derivatives, integrals, and infinite series, and constitutes a major part of modern university education. Historically, it has been referred to as 'the _____ of infinitesimals', or 'infinitesimal _____'. Most basically, _____ is the study of change, in the same way that geometry is the study of space.
   a. Test for Divergence
   b. Partial sum
   c. Hyperbolic angle
   d. Calculus

4. The mathematical concept of a _____ expresses the intuitive idea of deterministic dependence between two quantities, one of which is viewed as primary and the other as secondary. A _____ then is a way to associate a unique output for each input of a specified type, for example, a real number or an element of a given set.
   a. Grill
   b. Coherent
   c. Going up
   d. Function

5. Dependent variables and _____ refer to values that change in relationship to each other. The dependent variables are those that are observed to change in response to the _____. The _____ are those that are deliberately manipulated to invoke a change in the dependent variables.
   a. Operational confound
   b. One-factor-at-a-time method
   c. Experimental design diagram
   d. Independent variables

6. In mathematics, hyperbolic n-space, denoted H^n, is the maximally symmetric, simply connected, n-dimensional Riemannian manifold with constant sectional curvature −1. _____ is the principal example of a space exhibiting hyperbolic geometry. It can be thought of as the negative-curvature analogue of the n-sphere.
   a. Horocycle
   b. Margulis lemma
   c. Hyperbolic geometry
   d. Hyperbolic space

7. In mathematics, a _____ of a function of several variables is its derivative with respect to one of those variables with the others held constant. _____s are useful in vector calculus and differential geometry.

The _____ of a function f with respect to the variable x is written as f_x, $\partial_x f$, or $\partial f/\partial x$.

a. Critical number	b. Laplacian
c. Laplace invariant	d. Partial derivative

8. In mathematics, _____ and undefined are used to explain whether or not expressions have meaningful, sensible, and unambiguous values. Not all branches of mathematics come to the same conclusion.

The following expressions are undefined in all contexts, but remarks in the analysis section may apply.

a. Toy model	b. Plugging in
c. Defined	d. LHS

9. _____ is a fundamental construction of differential calculus and admits many possible generalizations within the fields of mathematical analysis, combinatorics, algebra, and geometry.

In real, complex, and functional analysis, _____s are generalized to functions of several real or complex variables and functions between topological vector spaces. An important case is the variational _____ in the calculus of variations.

a. Functional derivative	b. Metric derivative
c. Derivative	d. Lin-Tsien equation

10. In calculus, the _____ is a formula for the derivative of the composite of two functions.

In intuitive terms, if a variable, y, depends on a second variable, u, which in turn depends on a third variable, x, then the rate of change of y with respect to x can be computed as the rate of change of y with respect to u multiplied by the rate of change of u with respect to x. Schematically,

$$\frac{dy}{dx} = \frac{dy}{du} \cdot \frac{du}{dx}.$$

For an explanation of notation used in this section, see Function composition.

The _____ states that, under appropriate conditions,

$$(f \circ g)'(x) = f'(g(x))g'(x),$$

which in short form is written as

$$(f \circ g)' = f' \circ g \cdot g'.$$

Alternatively, in the Leibniz notation, the _____ is

$$\frac{dy}{dx} = \frac{dy}{du} \cdot \frac{du}{dx}.$$

In integration, the counterpart to the _____ is the substitution rule.

a. 1-center problem
c. Chain rule
b. 120-cell
d. Product rule

11. The _____ theory of wages, also referred to as the marginal revenue product of labor, is the change in total revenue earned by a firm that results from employing one more unit of labor. It is a neoclassical model that determines, under some conditions, the optimal number of workers to employ at an exogenously determined market wage rate. See Daniel S.

a. Coordinate rotations and reflections
c. Continuum hypothesis
b. Marginal revenue productivity
d. Continuous wave

12. _____ in economics refers to measures of output from production processes, per unit of input. Labor _____, for example, is typically measured as a ratio of output per labor-hour, an input. _____ may be conceived of as a measure of the technical or engineering efficiency of production.

a. 1-center problem
c. Productivity
b. 2-3 heap
d. 120-cell

13. _____ is a phenomenon which arises in the region of a continuous phase transition. Originally reported by Thomas Andrews in 1869 for the liquid-gas transition in carbon dioxide, many other examples have been discovered since. The phenomenon is most commonly demonstrated in binary fluid mixtures, such as methanol and cyclohexane.

a. Critical opalescence
c. Critical temperature
b. Fermi point
d. Percolation threshold

14. In mathematics, _____ and minima, known collectively as extrema, are the largest value or smallest value, that a function takes in a point either within a given neighbourhood or on the function domain in its entirety.

A real-valued function f' defined on the real line is said to have a local maximum point at the point x^*, if there exists some $\varepsilon > 0$, such that f≥ f½x − x^*| < ε. The value of the function at this point is called maximum of the function.

a. Descent
c. Maxima
b. Decimal system
d. Field

15. _____ are points in the domain of a function at which the function takes a largest value or smallest value, either within a given neighborhood or on the function domain in its entirety.

a. Test for Divergence
c. Calculus controversy
b. Minima
d. Maxima and minima

16. In mathematics, a _____ is a point in the domain of a function of two variables which is a stationary point but not a local extremum. At such a point, in general, the surface resembles a saddle that curves up in one direction, and curves down in a different direction. In terms of contour lines, a _____ can be recognized, in general, by a contour that appears to intersect itself.

a. Saddle point
b. 1-center problem
c. Gauss map
d. Gauss-Codazzi equations

17. In mathematics, maxima and _____, known collectively as extrema, are the largest value or smallest value, that a function takes in a point either within a given neighbourhood or on the function domain in its entirety.

A real-valued function f' defined on the real line is said to have a local maximum point at the point x^*, if there exists some $\varepsilon > 0$, such that f≥ f½x − x^* | < ε. The value of the function at this point is called maximum of the function.

a. Periodic function
b. Dirichlet integral
c. Calculus
d. Minima

18. In mathematics, a _____ is a point on the domain of a function where:

- one dimension: the derivative is equal to zero or a point where the function ceases to be differentiable.
- in general: there are two distinct concepts: either the derivative vanishes, or it is not of full rank; these agree in one dimension.

Note that in one dimension, a critical value or critical number x of function f is the domain element at which the derivative is zero or undefined, whereas the associated ordered pair is the _____. In higher dimensions a critical value is in the range whereas a _____ is in the domain.

There are two situations in which a point becomes a _____ of a function of one variable. The first of which is that the value of the derivative is equal to zero.

a. Decimal system
b. Derivative algebra
c. Critical point
d. Going up

19. In calculus, a branch of mathematics, the _____ determines whether a given stationary point of a function is a maximum or a minimum.

a. Christofides heuristics algorithm
b. Barrelled spaces
c. Cook reduction
d. Second-derivative test

20. In mathematical optimization, the method of _____ s is a method for finding the maximum/minimum of a function subject to constraints.

Chapter 15. Multivariable Calculus

For example if we want to solve:

$$\text{maximize } f(x, y)$$
$$\text{subject to } g(x, y) = c$$

We introduce a new variable called a _____ to rewrite the problem as:

$$\text{maximize } f(x, y) + \lambda(g(x, y) - c)$$

Solving this new unconstrained problem for x, y, and λ will give us the solution for our original constrained problem.

Introduction

Consider a two-dimensional case.

a. Radfar ratio
b. 120-cell
c. Lagrange multiplier
d. 1-center problem

21. In Fourier analysis, a _____ is a kind of linear operator, or transformation of functions. These operators multiply the Fourier coefficients of a function by a specified function, hence the name. Among the multipliers one can count some simple operators, such as translations and differentiation, but also some more complicated ones such as the convolutions, Hilbert transform, and others.

a. Reality condition
b. Modulated complex lapped transform
c. Fourier multiplier
d. Poisson summation formula

22. The method of _____ or ordinary _____ is used to solve overdetermined systems. _____ is often applied in statistical contexts, particularly regression analysis.

_____ can be interpreted as a method of fitting data.

a. Non-linear least squares
b. System equivalence
c. Rata Die
d. Least squares

23. In statistics, _____ is a form of regression analysis in which the relationship between one or more independent variables and another variable, called dependent variable, is modeled by a least squares function, called _____ equation. This function is a linear combination of one or more model parameters, called regression coefficients. A _____ equation with one independent variable represents a straight line.

a. Random variables
b. Kurtosis
c. Percentile rank
d. Linear regression

24. The _____ fallacy is an informal fallacy. It ascribes cause where none exists. The flaw is failing to account for natural fluctuations.

a. Regression
c. Depth

b. Degrees of freedom
d. Differential

25. In statistics, _____ is a collective name for techniques for the modeling and analysis of numerical data consisting of values of a dependent variable and of one or more independent variables. The dependent variable in the regression equation is modeled as a function of the independent variables, corresponding parameters, and an error term. The error term is treated as a random variable.

a. 120-cell
c. 1-center problem

b. 2-3 heap
d. Regression analysis

26. In mathematics, specifically in combinatorial commutative algebra, a convex lattice polytope P is called _____ if it has the following property: given any positive integer n, every lattice point of the dilation nP, obtained from P by scaling its vertices by the factor n and taking the convex hull of the resulting points, can be written as the sum of exactly n lattice points in P. This property plays an important role in the theory of toric varieties, where it corresponds to projective normality of the toric variety determined by P.

The simplex in R^k with the vertices at the origin and along the unit coordinate vectors is _____.

a. Polytetrahedron
c. Hypercube

b. Demihypercubes
d. Normal

27. A justification for choosing this criterion is given in properties below. This minimization problem has a unique solution, provided that the n columns of the matrix X are linearly independent, given by solving the _____

$$(X^\top X)\hat{\boldsymbol{\beta}} = X^\top \mathbf{y}.$$

The primary application of linear least squares is in data fitting. Given a set of m data points $y_1, y_2, \ldots, y_m$, consisting of experimentally measured values taken at m values $x_1, x_2, \ldots, x_m$ of an independent variable (x_i may be scalar or vector quantities), and given a model function $y = f(x, \boldsymbol{\beta})$, with $\boldsymbol{\beta} = (\beta_1, \beta_2, \ldots, \beta_n)$, it is desired to find the parameters β_j such that the model function fits 'best' the data.

a. Constraint optimization
c. Slack variable

b. Normal equations
d. Shekel function

28. In mathematics, a _____ is a statement that can be proved on the basis of explicitly stated or previously agreed assumptions.

a. Boolean function
c. Theorem

b. Disjunction introduction
d. Logical value

Chapter 15. Multivariable Calculus

29. A _____ typically refers to a class of handheld calculators that are capable of plotting graphs, solving simultaneous equations, and performing numerous other tasks with variables. Most popular _____s are also programmable, allowing the user to create customized programs, typically for scientific/engineering and education applications. Due to their large displays intended for graphing, they can also accommodate several lines of text and calculations at a time.

   a. Graphing calculator
   b. Bump mapping
   c. Support vector machines
   d. Genus

30. A _____ is a device for performing mathematical calculations, distinguished from a computer by having a limited problem solving ability and an interface optimized for interactive calculation rather than programming. _____s can be hardware or software, and mechanical or electronic, and are often built into devices such as PDAs or mobile phones.

Modern electronic _____s are generally small, digital, and usually inexpensive.

   a. 120-cell
   b. 1-center problem
   c. 2-3 heap
   d. Calculator

31. In signal processing, the _____ E_s of a continuous-time signal x

$$E_s = \langle x(t), x(t) \rangle = \int_{-\infty}^{\infty} |x(t)|^2 dt$$

_____ in this context is not, strictly speaking, the same as the conventional notion of _____ in physics and the other sciences. The two concepts are, however, closely related, and it is possible to convert from one to the other:

$$E = \frac{E_s}{Z} = \frac{1}{Z}\int_{-\infty}^{\infty} |x(t)|^2 dt$$

where Z represents the magnitude, in appropriate units of measure, of the load driven by the signal.

For example, if x

   a. Essential bandwidth
   b. Audio signal processing
   c. Energy
   d. Emphasis

32. The multiple integral is a type of definite integral extended to functions of more than one real variable, for example, fz = x^2 + y^2. The rectangular region at the bottom of the body is the domain of integration, while the surface is the graph of the two-variable function to be integrated.

Introduction

Just as the definite integral of a positive function of one variable represents the area of the region between the graph of the function and the x-axis, the _____ of a positive function of two variables represents the volume of the region between the surface defined by the function and the plane which contains its domain.

Chapter 15. Multivariable Calculus

a. Solid of revolution
b. Risch algorithm
c. Signed measure
d. Double integral

33. In mathematics, an _____, or central tendency of a data set refers to a measure of the 'middle' or 'expected' value of the data set. There are many different descriptive statistics that can be chosen as a measurement of the central tendency of the data items.

An _____ is a single value that is meant to typify a list of values.

a. A posteriori
b. A Mathematical Theory of Communication
c. Average
d. A chemical equation

34. In commutative algebra, the notions of an element _____ over a ring, and of an _____ extension of rings, are a generalization of the notions in field theory of an element being algebraic over a field, and of an algebraic extension of fields.

The special case of greatest interest in number theory is that of complex numbers _____ over the ring of integers Z.

The term ring will be understood to mean commutative ring with a unit.

a. Arc length
b. Integral
c. Antidifferentiation
d. Integral test for convergence

35. In calculus, an antiderivative, primitive or indefinite integral of a function f is a function F whose derivative is equal to f. The process of solving for antiderivatives is _____. Antiderivatives are related to definite integrals through the fundamental theorem of calculus, and provide a convenient means for calculating the definite integrals of many functions.

a. Indefinite integral
b. Integration by parts operator
c. Arc length
d. Antidifferentiation

36. In complex analysis, a branch of mathematics, the _____ of a complex-valued function g is a function whose complex derivative is g. More precisely, given an open set U in the complex plane and a function $g : U \to \mathbb{C}$, the _____ of g is a function $f : U \to \mathbb{C}$ that satisfies $\frac{df}{dz} = g$.

As such, this concept is the complex-variable version of the _____ of a real-valued function.

a. Integration by parts
b. Integral
c. Indefinite integral
d. Antiderivative

37. _____ is a core concept of basic mathematics, specifically in the fields of infinitesimal calculus and mathematical analysis. Given a function f

Chapter 15. Multivariable Calculus

$$\int_a^b f(x)\,dx,$$

is equal to the area of a region in the xy-plane bounded by the graph of f, the x-axis, and the vertical lines x = a and x = b, with areas below the x-axis being subtracted.

The term 'integral' may also refer to the notion of antiderivative, a function F whose derivative is the given function f.

a. OMAC
b. Epigraph
c. Apex
d. Integration

38. The _____ is a function in mathematics. The application of this function to a value x is written as ex. Equivalently, this can be written in the form e^x, where e is a mathematical constant, the base of the natural logarithm, which equals approximately 2.718281828, and is also known as Euler's number.

a. A chemical equation
b. Exponential function
c. Area hyperbolic functions
d. A Mathematical Theory of Communication

39. The _____ of any solid, plasma, vacuum or theoretical object is how much three-dimensional space it occupies, often quantified numerically. One-dimensional figures and two-dimensional shapes are assigned zero _____ in the three-dimensional space. _____ is presented as ml or cm³.

_____s of straight-edged and circular shapes are calculated using arithmetic formulae.

a. Stress-energy tensor
b. Thermodynamic limit
c. Volume
d. Cauchy momentum equation

40. In mathematics, specifically in topology, a _____ is a two-dimensional manifold. The most familiar examples are those that arise as the boundaries of solid objects in ordinary three-dimensional Euclidean space, EÂ³. On the other hand, there are also more exotic _____s, that are so 'contorted' that they cannot be embedded in three-dimensional space at all.

a. Homoeoid
b. Surface
c. Cross-cap
d. Standard torus

41. In mathematics, an _____ in the sense of ring theory is a subring $\mathcal{O}$ of a ring R that satisfies the conditions

1. R is a ring which is a finite-dimensional algebra over the rational number field $\mathbb{Q}$
2. $\mathcal{O}$ spans R over $\mathbb{Q}$, so that $\mathbb{Q}\mathcal{O} = R$, and
3. $\mathcal{O}$ is a lattice in R.

The third condition can be stated more accurately, in terms of the extension of scalars of R to the real numbers, embedding R in a real vector space. In less formal terms, additively $\mathcal{O}$ should be a free abelian group generated by a basis for R over $\mathbb{Q}$.

The leading example is the case where R is a number field K and $\mathcal{O}$ is its ring of integers. In algebraic number theory there are examples for any K other than the rational field of proper subrings of the ring of integers that are also _____s.

a. Efficiency
c. Algebraic
b. Order
d. Annihilator

42. _____, denoted I

A time series is integrated of order 0 if

$$\sum_{k=0}^{\infty} |\gamma_k^2| < \infty$$

- it admits a moving average representation with $k=0$
- This is a necessary, but not sufficient condition for a stationary process. Therefore, all stationary processes are , but not all processes are stationary. Most UK textbooks ignore this distinction.

A time series is integrated of order P if:

- $(1-L)^P X_t$ is integrated of order 0

This says that a process is Integrated if taking repeated differences yields a stationary process.

$(1-L)$ is the First difference operator, ie: $(1-L)X_t = X_t - X_{t-1} = \Delta X$

For a discussion of this notation see Lag operator.

a. Anomaly time series
c. Univariate distribution
b. Omnibus tests
d. Order of Integration

43. _____ and independent variables refer to values that change in relationship to each other. The _____ are those that are observed to change in response to the independent variables. The independent variables are those that are deliberately manipulated to invoke a change in the _____.

a. Yates analysis
c. Steiner system
b. Round robin test
d. Dependent variables

44. A real-valued function f defined on the real line is said to have a _____ point at the point x∗, if there exists some ε > 0, such that f when x − x∗ < ε.

a. Binomial series
c. Hyperbolic angle
b. Calculus controversy
d. Local maximum

ANSWER KEY

Chapter 1
1. d   2. d   3. b   4. b   5. d   6. d   7. a   8. a   9. d   10. a
11. a   12. b   13. d   14. d   15. d   16. a   17. b   18. b   19. d   20. d
21. d   22. d   23. d   24. d   25. d   26. d   27. b   28. d   29. d   30. a
31. d   32. c   33. d   34. d   35. a   36. b   37. a   38. a   39. d   40. a
41. c   42. a   43. d

Chapter 2
1. b   2. c   3. d   4. d   5. d   6. b   7. d   8. d   9. c   10. d
11. d   12. b   13. d   14. d   15. d   16. d   17. b   18. d   19. c   20. b
21. c   22. a   23. c   24. d   25. d   26. d   27. c   28. b   29. d   30. d
31. d   32. c   33. c   34. c   35. d   36. d   37. d   38. b   39. d   40. b
41. d   42. d   43. b   44. d   45. d   46. d   47. d

Chapter 3
1. c   2. d   3. a   4. a   5. c   6. b   7. c   8. d   9. c   10. d
11. d   12. d   13. a   14. d   15. d   16. d   17. d   18. c   19. d   20. b
21. d   22. c   23. d   24. d   25. d

Chapter 4
1. a   2. c   3. d   4. d   5. c   6. d   7. b   8. d   9. b   10. d
11. d   12. d   13. d   14. a   15. c   16. c   17. d   18. b   19. a   20. c
21. d   22. a   23. b   24. d   25. d   26. c   27. a   28. b   29. b   30. d
31. c

Chapter 5
1. b   2. d   3. c   4. b   5. b   6. d   7. a   8. b   9. d   10. d
11. d   12. b   13. d   14. b   15. b   16. d   17. d   18. d

Chapter 6
1. a   2. d   3. c   4. b   5. d   6. d   7. a   8. c   9. c   10. d
11. c   12. d   13. a   14. d   15. a   16. d   17. a   18. a   19. a   20. d
21. a

Chapter 7
1. d   2. d   3. a   4. b   5. d   6. d   7. d   8. d   9. d   10. d
11. c   12. c   13. d   14. c   15. d   16. d   17. a   18. b   19. d   20. d
21. c   22. b   23. b   24. d   25. a   26. a   27. b   28. d   29. d   30. d
31. a   32. d

Chapter 8
1. d   2. c   3. d   4. d   5. a   6. d   7. c   8. d   9. d   10. a
11. d   12. d   13. d   14. d   15. d   16. d   17. a   18. a   19. d   20. a
21. d   22. c   23. d   24. b   25. d   26. d   27. c   28. d   29. d   30. b
31. b   32. d   33. b   34. b   35. d   36. d   37. d   38. d

Chapter 9
1. d	2. d	3. d	4. d	5. c	6. a	7. b	8. d	9. d	10. a
11. d	12. a	13. a	14. a	15. a	16. b	17. d	18. a	19. d	20. d
21. c									

Chapter 10
1. d	2. d	3. d	4. a	5. a	6. d	7. b	8. a	9. d	10. d
11. d	12. d	13. a	14. d	15. d	16. d	17. b	18. d	19. d	20. c
21. c	22. d	23. d	24. d	25. d	26. c	27. a	28. a	29. d	30. b
31. d	32. a	33. c	34. b	35. b	36. d	37. d	38. b	39. d	40. d
41. a	42. d	43. d	44. d	45. b	46. c	47. c			

Chapter 11
1. d	2. d	3. d	4. a	5. d	6. d	7. d	8. d	9. c	10. c
11. d	12. a	13. d	14. d	15. d	16. b	17. d	18. a	19. d	20. d
21. b	22. d	23. c	24. d	25. d	26. d	27. d	28. b		

Chapter 12
1. d	2. a	3. a	4. c	5. d	6. d	7. d	8. d	9. d	10. b
11. c	12. c	13. a	14. d	15. d	16. a	17. a	18. d	19. a	20. b
21. d	22. c	23. d	24. c	25. b	26. c	27. d	28. b	29. d	30. d
31. d	32. c	33. d	34. d	35. c	36. b	37. b	38. d	39. a	40. c

Chapter 13
1. d	2. b	3. b	4. d	5. b	6. a	7. d	8. d	9. a	10. d
11. d	12. a	13. d	14. a	15. a	16. a	17. d	18. d	19. b	20. d
21. d	22. a	23. a	24. d	25. c	26. c	27. d	28. d	29. a	30. b
31. d	32. d	33. b	34. d	35. b	36. c	37. d	38. d	39. a	40. a
41. d	42. d								

Chapter 14
1. d	2. b	3. b	4. d	5. d	6. d	7. b	8. c	9. d	10. d
11. d	12. d	13. c	14. c	15. d	16. b	17. a	18. b	19. d	20. b
21. d	22. d	23. c	24. a						

Chapter 15
1. d	2. a	3. d	4. d	5. d	6. d	7. d	8. c	9. c	10. c
11. b	12. c	13. a	14. c	15. d	16. a	17. d	18. c	19. d	20. c
21. c	22. d	23. d	24. a	25. d	26. d	27. b	28. c	29. a	30. d
31. c	32. d	33. c	34. b	35. d	36. d	37. d	38. b	39. c	40. b
41. b	42. d	43. d	44. d